Magazine Editors
Talk to Writers

Wiley Books for Writers Series

Literary Agents: What They Do, How They Do It, and How to Find and Work with the Right One for You, by Michael Larsen

Book Editors Talk to Writers, by Judy Mandell

The Elements of Storytelling: How to Write Compelling Fiction, by Peter Rubie

Networking at Writer's Conferences: From Contacts to Contracts, by Steven D. Spratt and Lee G. Spratt

Magazine Editors Talk to Writers

JUDY MANDELL

JOHN WILEY & SONS, INC.

New York · Chichester · Brisbane · Toronto · Singapore

For Jerry, Pam, Scott,
Kim, Jim, Elizabeth,
Joshua, Zachary, and littlest
but not least, Peekanut

This text is printed on acid-free paper.

Copyright © 1996 by Judy Mandell
Published by John Wiley & Sons, Inc.

Library of Congress Cataloging-in-Publication Data

Mandell, Judy.
    Magazine editors talk to writers / Judy Mandell.
        p.   cm.—(Wiley books for writers series)
    ISBN 0-471-11991-1
    1. Feature writing.   2. Journalism—Authorship.   3. Periodicals
editors—Interviews.   I. Title.   II. Series.
PN4784.F37M36   1996
808'.06605—dc20   95-52686

Printed in the United States of America

10 9 8 7 6 5 4 3 2 1

Contents

Preface

Several years ago, the editor of a major women's magazine agreed to an interview for an article I was writing. I sent her a letter confirming the time and date of our scheduled meeting. Two weeks later I received a response that read: "Dear Writer, Thank you for your query. Unfortunately we cannot use your article. Good luck in placing it elsewhere."

My letter was obviously mistaken for an unsolicited query and returned, unread, by an assistant editor. I was not totally surprised. After more than twenty-five years as a freelance writer, I'd received innumerable form rejection letters from magazine editors. I occasionally suspected that my queries were returned unread and wondered whether this was a common phenomenon. Was unsolicited material often rejected and returned unread? This incident spurred me to investigate the relationship between freelance writers and magazine editors.

To research the problem for a *Writer's Digest* magazine article, I interviewed a half-dozen magazine editors who claimed that, even at top magazines, almost every query is read by someone. Editors need good ideas, good material, and good writers for their magazines. Although editors are "up to their eyeballs" acquiring, editing, and publishing articles, and don't have time for mediocre queries from unknown writers, freelancers can spark an editor's interest with a terrific query. They can break in and get published if they do their homework, play by the rules, and write smart.

The success of my *Writer's Digest* article motivated me to write *Magazine Editors Talk to Writers*, for which I interviewed forty top magazine editors.

My goal for *Magazine Editors Talk to Writers* is to help writers get published by better understanding how magazine editors think and how magazine publishing works. I wrote the book with the assumption that my readers know little of publishing. Most of the information should be valuable to sophisticated free-lancers as well as beginning writers, and of interest to anyone who is curious about magazine publishing.

Each chapter of *Magazine Editors Talk to Writers* begins with a short bio of the editor, covers a different topic, and includes a brief description of the editor's magazine—its founding date and present circulation. Additional material about the magazine as a market for freelance writers is usually included in the text as well.

Magazine Editors Talk to Writers is divided in two parts: Part One: What Every Writer Wants to Know (But May Be Afraid to Ask) and Part Two: The Magazines.

Although every magazine publisher has its own preferences and requirements, there are many across-the-board rules of etiquette and submission procedure.

The information in Part One should interest all readers. I asked editors in this section to talk about magazine publishing in general—the lingo, keys to breaking in at the top magazines, the evolution of men's and women's magazines, professional etiquette for writers, magazines and the information superhighway, the future of publishing, and so on. When appropriate, I also slipped in questions about how to get published in the editor's own magazine.

Part Two includes a selection of top magazine editors who represent a variety of freelance markets. Here readers can seek out chapters on areas that interest them, although much of the material in this section applies to most writers.

I posed to editors what I thought were freelance writers' most-asked questions and problems: How do you usually acquire articles? Do you look at material that comes in over the transom? How can writers break in at top magazines? How can writers determine the right idea and tone for a particular magazine? How can they figure out hot topics? Should writers always query a magazine first? Is it okay to send in a completed manuscript? Is it important to send the query to a specific editor (by name)? How do most editors feel about multiple submissions? How long should writers expect to wait for a response? How does the editorial process generally work once an article has been assigned?

I asked editors to reveal "the truth" about magazine publishing. What do editors want from writers? What qualifies editors to do all the things they do? Are editors really necessary? Do editors ever steal ideas from queries that were rejected? Is it helpful for a freelance writer to retain an agent? What are the worst things that writers do or don't do? What endears certain writers to you? What are your pet peeves? How can a writer become a regular contributor to a magazine?

Most chapters end with pet peeves and advice to writers so that readers can quickly find the "inside scoop" and compare editors' points of view.

I used a question-and-answer format because it reveals the editor's persona and because readers can easily locate topics of interest.

Because jargon is ubiquitous in magazine publishing, I placed Todd Balf's chapter on magazine publishing lingo at the beginning so that readers can decipher the distinctive terms found throughout this book.

Acknowledgments

To the wonderful editors
who graciously gave me so much of their precious time.
Thank you.

Thank you for the explanations, the exhortations, the revelations, the dedication, and the inspiration.

Despite your overwhelming workloads and production deadlines,
you eagerly talked to me.

For that I am grateful.

And thanks to PJ Dempsey, Senior Editor, and to Chris Jackson, Assistant Editor, at John Wiley & Sons.

Part One

What Every Magazine
Writer Wants to Know
(But May Be Afraid to Ask)

Magazine Publishing Lingo

The Masthead, Slush, Over the Transom, Lead Times, Kill Fees, Copyright, Deadlines, and More

TODD BALF, FULL-TIME FREELANCE WRITER AND CONSULTING EDITOR

Former Senior Editor at _Outside_
Beverly, Massachusetts

TODD BALF is a full-time freelance writer for _Travel & Leisure_, _Outside_, _Self_, _GQ_, _Men's Journal_, and _Yankee_. He also edits and assigns articles for _Outside_'s sports news column for the _Record_. Balf's college major was English, with an emphasis on journalism. After graduation, he worked as a fact-checker at _Esquire_. After two years, he went to _Ultra Sport_ magazine as associate editor, and then to _Outside_ magazine as a senior editor. In 1989 he left _Outside_ to freelance full-time.

☐ **What is the magazine masthead?**
The masthead is the lineup of editors, usually published near the front of every magazine. It's hierarchical. It's political as well. Each magazine's masthead differs slightly, but usually starts with the publisher on the top line. Farther down the masthead are senior-level editors, which may include the deputy editor, executive editor, editor in chief, managing editor, senior editors, and associate editors. Assistant editors and interns follow. Contributing editors are often listed last. They are not actually editors, but writers who contribute on a regular basis.

□ What are freelance writers?

Freelance writers are subcontractors to a magazine. They are not on staff. They are assigned an article that they deliver on a specified date. Freelancers are free to work for any publication. *Webster's International Dictionary* defines a freelance writer as "a writer who writes stories or articles for the open market with long-term commitments to no one publisher or periodical."

□ What are in-house writers?

People who write exclusively for the magazine on whose masthead they are listed.

□ What is an editor?

An editor is on the staff of a magazine. Editors generate story ideas and assign those stories to writers, either in-house or freelance. When the articles come in, editors line-edit or do whatever it takes to make those stories good.

□ What is an assignment?

When an editor contracts with a writer to do a story with a given number of words for a specific amount of money by a certain date.

□ What is a byline?

A byline is the author's name; it usually appears at the beginning of a full feature story.

□ What is a tag line?

A tag line is the author's name usually printed at the end of an abbreviated piece.

□ What is a pen name?

It's a name other than your real one. Writers use pen names for different purposes. Sometimes they use pen names because they write for a number of magazines that are similar to one another.

□ What is over the transom?

Over-the-transom material is unsolicited.

□ What is slush?

Slush is the name given to unsolicited stories sent to magazines. Every editor receives slush. Editors may read these stories and decide whether they are useful to the magazine. Generally, the bigger the magazine, the less chance that an unsolicited story will be published. Magazines vary as to how conscientious they are about reading slush material. Unfortunately, a lot of stories go unread or if they are read, they're not read with as fine an eye as they could be. Queries are in a different category and are not usually considered slush.

□ What is a query!

A query is a story idea that has been written by either an in-house staff writer or a freelance writer. It is a shortened version of what an article will look like, and lets an editor decide if she wants to pursue that story. A query is universally regarded as a written piece. It is usually one page, because the rule of thumb is that you should be able to tell a story and sell a story in one page, no matter the complexity. Editors prefer queries to full manuscripts and so they are more likely to be read if they come in over the transom. If an editor is leery of an unproven writer, but likes the query, he might ask the person to write the piece on speculation.

□ What does it mean to write an article "on speculation" or on "spec"?

The writer completes a story and submits it to the magazine with the hope that it will be accepted. If it is, he or she will be paid for it. The writer does not, in this case, have a contract or a promise of publication.

□ What is a kill fee?

If the magazine that assigned a story decides not to run it after it has been delivered, editors generally give the writer 20 percent to 25 percent of the fee originally agreed upon. That's called a kill fee, since they essentially have killed the story. Writers usually receive back the rights to the story and can peddle it elsewhere.

□ What does it mean to pitch a story?

That is usually a verbal, rather than a written approach. It's when you've got an editor on the phone and are trying to sell a piece or an idea for a story.

□ What are clips?

Clips are published pieces (usually copies) from other magazines or newspapers that are usually sent by first-time writers with the query.

□ What is a SASE?

It's a self-addressed, stamped envelope. Writers should always include a SASE with a query if they want a reply.

□ What are multiple submissions?

When a freelance writer sends a query or story to a number of different magazines.

□ What is slanting a story? Is that the same as the story's angle?

To slant a story to write it with the magazine's audience in mind. For example, you would slant a story one way for a men's magazine and another way for a women's magazine. The angle is similar to the slant.

□ What is shaping a piece?

Shaping a piece means giving it magazine attributes—for example, a strong lead (beginning) that will bring the reader in and a strong narrative to tell the story.

□ What is lead time?

Lead time is the amount of time—days, weeks, or months, depending on the publishing schedule of the magazine—that is needed between gathering the information to be included in the issue and actually putting it into production. It's usually several months before a magazine issue is put into production.

□ What is a deadline?

The deadline is the date on which an editor wants an article delivered by a writer.

□ What is a line edit?

This is what an editor does to every story. Line editing is reading for content and narrative flow.

□ What are revisions?

After an editor has read and line-edited a story, it is sent back to the writer with requested changes. Those changes are revisions.

□ What is copyediting?

This is editing for punctuation and content and is done after revisions have been made by the writer.

□ What are galleys?

Galleys are the actual typeset pages from the magazine, as opposed to the computer-printed manuscript that the writer submitted to the editor. Although the story is not in its final version, it appears as it will be seen in the magazine. There are usually four or five rounds of galleys in which corrections are made. Fact-checking corrections, copyediting corrections, and editing additions are made in galleys.

□ What is copyright?

Copyright is the law that protects your words and your writing. There are legal avenues that you could follow if someone were to infringe on that copyright. According to Ronald Goldfarb and Gail Ross in their book *The Writer's Lawyer* (Times Books), author's copyright of a magazine article consists of a number of separate rights. The freelance writer wants to offer as few rights to the publisher as possible. Magazines commonly buy first North American serial rights. In that case, a writer gives the publisher the right to be the first magazine to publish the article in North America. After publication, the writer may do whatever he or she wants with the piece and keep the proceeds.

□ **What are cover lines?**

They are one-line descriptions of articles printed on magazine covers. Their purpose is to entice readers to pick up the magazine.

□ **What is the well?**

The well is the center of the magazine, where the centerfold appears.

□ **What are consumer magazines?**

Consumer magazines are the general-interest magazines you see on newsstands.

□ **What are trade magazines?**

Trade magazines are very narrow-niche magazines that are targeted specifically to certain occupations or professions, such as *Electricity Today* for electricians or the *ABA Journal* for lawyers. They are usually available only by subscription and are not sold on newsstands.

□ **What are service stories?**

Service stories are useful as well as entertaining. They usually cover the craze of the moment, which is what most magazines want. An example would be "How to Get in Shape."

□ **What is a profile?**

It's a story about a person.

□ **What is *Writer's Market*?**

Writer's Market is an annually published guide for writers that offers magazine listings, editors' names, pay scales, and more. It's a great tool for beginning writers.

□ **Do you have advice for writers in search of a magazine publisher?**

Know the magazine publishing business. Read books and magazines. Work for a magazine, whether it's an internship during college or a job after graduation. You will develop contacts and a networking system that you can rely on as a writer for many years. I think that's the biggest difference between writers who regularly publish and those who don't.

Freelance Writers' Most-Asked Questions

How Can Writers Break In at Top Magazines? How Can Writers Know What's Hot? Do Editors Steal Writers' Ideas? and More

MYRNA BLYTH, EDITOR IN CHIEF
AND PUBLISHING DIRECTOR
Ladies' Home Journal
New York

MYRNA BLYTH majored in literature and theater at Bennington College, where she worked on the literary magazine and various other publications. After graduation, her first job in publishing was at *Ingenue*, a magazine for teens. From *Ingenue*, Blyth went to *Family Health* as a senior editor, and then to *Family Circle*, where she worked her way up from fiction editor to executive editor. In 1981 Blyth left *Family Circle* to become editor in chief of *Ladies' Home Journal*.

Founded in 1883, *Ladies' Home Journal* is the oldest women's magazine published in its original format. "The *Journal* is a contemporary magazine that reflects women today," says Blyth. The magazine has a monthly circulation of 5 million and a readership of 17 million.

□ **How do you usually acquire articles?**

Ideas come from the staff and from outside contributors. Some pieces are staff written and some are written by outside contributors.

□ **Do you assign many articles so that you have a large inventory to fall back on?**

Not anymore. Editors are very careful these days. They don't want big, fat inventories. There are very tight budget constraints on all aspects of magazine publishing today, including the writing.

□ **What percent of *Ladies' Home Journal* articles are written by outside contributors?**

About 75 percent.

□ **Do you have a stable of outside freelancers upon whom you depend?**

Yes. We depend on four or five contributing editors.

□ **Do you look at material that comes in over the transom?**

In some departments. For example, we look carefully at material submitted to the "A Woman Today" section. These are essays written by women describing their own experiences.

□ **What's the best way for a first-time writer to be published in *Ladies' Home Journal*?**

The best way to be published is to write a query that is provocative enough that an editor would ask you to try the piece on spec. But the chance of that happening is not great because we usually generate ideas ourselves and assign them to writers we know.

□ **How can writers break in at top magazines?**

Be very familiar with the magazine. Tell a story that's unique. Offer an idea that is very focused for the magazine. It could be a local story that has national appeal. A query that says, "I'd like to do a piece on women's friendship" is no way to get an editor's interest.

□ **Are there hot topics?**

Yes, but they change quickly. A hot topic today won't be a hot topic in a year. A writer who is aware of what's going on in the world will figure it out. She will get it in the zeitgeist. Hot topics are what interest people now and what's going to interest them in the future. Freelancers who can sense the beginning of a wave of interest are usually the good writers. With luck, an editor on the magazine staff will recognize a hot topic.

□ **Do most magazines provide writer's guidelines?**

Yes. But studying the magazine is the best guideline of all.

□ **Should a writer query a magazine first or send in a completed manuscript?**

It is more sensible to write a very good query and perhaps the beginning of a manuscript. That way, you're telling an editor specifically what you want to write, while offering some assurance that you will actually achieve your goal. The editor might not like a portion of the completed manuscript and reject the whole thing. The only exceptions to that rule are a personal narrative or an "as-told-to." In those cases, you can sell the whole thing because that *is* the story.

□ **Are all queries read by someone at your magazine?**

Yes. Queries are read by someone, but not by a top editor. They're usually read by an editorial assistant or an associate editor.

□ **Is it important to send the query to a named editor?**

Yes. It shows that you know the masthead of the magazine and that you care enough to focus your query. However, even if it's sent to a named editor, a query may be read and screened by that editor's associate or assistant.

□ **What is the best way to submit a query?**

Be professional. Use letterhead. An unknown writer must be very careful. As in any job query, it wouldn't look good to send a letter on a piece of plain paper. Always include a self-addressed, stamped envelope to insure a response if sending a query over the transom. Writers should have patience. Freelancers should wait at least four weeks for a response from an editor, especially for a story that is not timely.

□ **Is it okay to fax a query?**

Only if there's an immediacy to the query. If there's no time factor, a fax is unappealing.

□ **Is it okay to call editors about a timely story?**

Only if there's a timeliness and it's a real story.

□ **How do you feel about multiple submissions?**

It's annoying to an editor to discover that a competitor has bought a story that he or she has decided to assign.

□ **Do editors ever steal ideas from queries that were rejected?**

Most ideas are pretty obvious. Many people have the same idea at the same time. Years ago, when I was at *Family Circle*, a writer suggested an article about a Williamsburg Christmas. Someone was already doing that piece. The writer was very upset.

An editor may like an idea, but feel that the writer isn't capable of writing the story. In that case, the editor may pay the freelancer for the idea and assign the story to an experienced writer. That's our policy.

□ What are your pet peeves about freelance writers?

Writers who suggest an article that's been in a recent issue. Or writers who offer an article that isn't at all appropriate to the magazine.

□ How can a writer become a regular contributor to a magazine?

Be a terrific writer and write pieces that the magazine wants to use.

□ Do you have advice for freelance writers who want to be published in top magazines?

Try to be published in a magazine that will publish you. Work for publications for which your level of experience is most appropriate. It's very foolish to spend your time making queries to major national magazines when you could possibly write for your local paper. I'm not saying that you'll never write for major national magazines, but instead of spending your time writing and rewriting queries, it would make a lot more sense to get an article in the local paper every week. From that, a writer can build the writing experience, not the trying-to-get-an-assignment experience. What we really want is writers who can write.

Be smart. I have given speeches to freelance writers, giving them real advice. And then someone raises his hand and asks, "Does everything have to be typed double-spaced?" Of course it does! Know the rules.

Present editors with clips of your writing material to show that you can write and have already been successfully published.

Have a good story to tell. We are always looking for good stories.

Offer a unique story and a unique style of writing.

Freelance writers get much too caught up in the querying—in the business of being a freelance writer instead of in the business of being a communicator. Writers should be more concerned with communicating a piece to the reading public than trying to communicate an idea to an editor.

□ What is your philosophy of the relationship between freelance writers and editors?

Freelance writers and editors are like singles bars. The guys are always looking for the girls, the women are always looking for the men, and nobody understands why, if so many people are looking, nobody ever gets it together. In truth, if somebody sends us a wonderful query and it's a terrific story, it will get noticed. If it doesn't get noticed, it's probably because it's not a terrific enough story.

A smart editor is going to find the smart story.

Magazine Editors

Who Are They? What Do They Do? What
Qualifies Them to Do All the Things They
Do? What Do They Want from Freelance
Writers? How Does the Editorial Process
Work Once an Article Has Been Assigned?
and More

CLAUDIA VALENTINO, EDITOR AND WRITER

Former Managing Editor at *Penthouse*
and *American Health*
Former Articles Editor at *Popular Science*
New York

CLAUDIA VALENTINO graduated from New York University with a
degree in magazine journalism. Her first job in publishing was at *Penthouse Magazine*, where she quickly climbed the ranks from editorial assistant to managing editor. After 5¹/₂ years, she moved to *American Health*
as managing editor and later to *Popular Science* as articles editor. Although Valentino is currently taking time off to write fiction, she is a
magazine publishing maven. "I love the business," says Valentino. "Magazines are wonderful. At their best, they're like no other art form."

☐ **What do the various editorial titles listed on the masthead mean?**
Associate editors generally handle shorter pieces and less complex articles.

Acquisitions and articles editors have generally comparable positions. They acquire articles and seek out writers. A good acquisitions or articles editor can assess a writer just by looking at clips, queries, or from a phone conversation.

Senior editors are usually acquiring editors. They often have a beat or special focus such as fiction, entertainment, or special projects, which is not always evident from the masthead.

The *managing editor* usually deals with the complex trafficking of materials among departments (art, editorial, production, and advertising) and keeps the magazine staff on schedule. A monthly magazine staff works on no fewer than three issues at a time, and they often get wrapped up in individual projects. The managing editor reminds everyone up and down the masthead about upcoming issues. This is not just a policeman's job. A managing editor of the best sort can create an environment in which staff members do their best work.

The job of *editor in chief* varies from magazine to magazine. Some editors in chief are heavily involved in commissioning, editing, and design making decisions. At the other end of the spectrum, others are figureheads. Look at Grace Mirabella, former editor of *Vogue*. Her relationship to the fashion world creates an identity for the magazine that was actually named for her, *Mirabella*.

An *executive editor* deals with business matters and often fills in for the editor in chief.

Contributing editors are the primary stable of writers that a magazine relies on. They are often called on by the editors to brainstorm.

□ What business decisions do editors make?
An editor's main task, publishing articles, *is* a business decision. Cover lines are definitely a business decision. An editor could completely muffle the impact of a wonderful piece that he has gone to great lengths to get and has paid a lot of money for by not selling it correctly on the cover. It would be as if he never published the article.

Editors are in a very competitive situation. The reader is under no obligation to read a particular magazine. Every issue must sparkle. Each piece has to work. These editorial decisions affect newsstand sales. If newsstand sales are not good, guess what? You're out!

□ What is one of a magazine editor's most difficult tasks?
Handling controversial material. It's expensive, it eats up space, and it's dangerous. But calculated risks are worth it. They help magazines stay fresh.

□ What defines a successful editor?
I define success as fluency within the craft. An editor should be able to think on his or her feet. A good editor understands cost and time factors as well as the

mechanics involved and naturally incorporates that understanding into creative decisions.

An editor must be able to do several contradictory things simultaneously, including being true to the identity of the magazine while coming up with something fresh. These can be warring objectives. The challenge is to keep a magazine fresh without violating the magazine's identity and the magazine's pact with the reader.

□ Should the editor's philosophy be reflected in the magazine?

In a consumer magazine, only the editor's professional philosophy about the craft of magazine making should be reflected. An editor won't use the magazine as a mouthpiece for his point of view. He's working in service to a concept, in a broad sense. He may pursue his enthusiasms in service to his readers, but he ought to remain aware of what he's doing.

□ Are editors really necessary?

Yes. An editor is like a costumer. He prepares work for presentation to the public. An editor positions a piece. An editor helps the writer hit a particular nail on the head. Editors possess many strategies to help writers. A writer is often too close to his work. He may have a blind spot, which the editor can clarify. The writer's job is to be familiar with his subject. The editor's job is to be thoroughly familiar with his magazine.

Writers may not understand what goes on internally at a publication. A lot of requirements must be satisfied for a piece to fit in a particular issue. That's why editorial assistance has to happen. There's no doing without it.

□ Do editors also work with less experienced writers who need help?

I've taken them on. Other editors will, too, if they see promise. Initially I may move such writers to less ambitious projects or pare down proposals to give them a fighting chance.

□ How should a writer view his or her editor?

The editor is the writer's means to getting published and paid for his work. Writers ought to learn as much as they can from each editor they work with. Writers should accept, indeed welcome, the involvement of their editor, especially when they're starting out. A magazine piece is a team effort.

□ How should writers deal with editors?

Don't become a master of the query letter and then a disaster on follow-through. Writers should be prepared before they send a query and before every phone call to their editor.

□ How should editors deal with writers?

Don't be authoritarian. Value a writer's talent, good sense, and discipline. If these qualities are there they'll be evident even in less experienced writers and should be cultivated. An editor should be clear in his own mind, and to the writer, about what he wants. He must be a bit of a matchmaker in finding the right writer for the right project. No matter how good a query sounds, the editor must determine in advance and correctly whether the writer can deliver the goods.

□ What are the worst things that writers do?

The worst things writers do are the following: not researching the magazine sufficiently; handing in stories that are too long, too short, or poorly reported; missing deadlines without explanation; being poor craftsmen; and not doing sufficient reporting and research before preparing the query.

□ How much research should a writer do for the query?

Many writers think that they shouldn't do extensive research or reporting before they are certain that they'll get the assignment. That's wrong. If they do 60 percent of the reporting to formulate a query, they'll probably get the assignment and 60 percent of their work will be done. If they get a rejection, the reporting and research that they've done is like money in the bank. They can reshape the query for another magazine. Moreover, they won't have been rejected for reasons that will reflect badly on them.

□ How do you view queries?

The query is indicative of many things. People ask if they should send clips with their query. I say, Yes, of course. But don't forget that your query is also a clip. The query is the first unedited writing sample a writer sends to an editor. The query is a dead giveaway of the writer's ability to analyze a topic and to pass along those realizations to another person for that particular editor's magazine. The query is essentially a magazine piece in miniature.

□ How does the editorial process generally work once an article has been assigned?

While the author is writing his article, staff, time, and money are already being invested in what he has promised to do. The art department may prepare a preliminary layout on the basis of the editor's description of the piece. Space is allotted in the magazine lineup. When the article arrives, the editor circulates it to the top editors for comments. The writer and the editor handle questions together. The editor then edits the piece. The article is again circulated in hard copy or electronically to the top editors and to the art department in its edited form. Very early on the research department has a go at it. Some magazines want research and reporting materials sent with the manuscript. They may want the writer to xerox all backup materials—people she has spoken to, telephone numbers, news clips, and so on. Some magazines will want the writer to answer questions to assure them that the information in the piece is solid. An attorney may review the manuscript for possible libel issues and inaccuracies to ward off legal trouble. Files of all this material are kept for years, especially at leading publications. The writer is expected to make himself available to researchers, copy chiefs, and lawyers to move a piece along. Once the piece is fact-checked and legally vetted, the copy department will edit it for spelling, grammatical errors, and house style. This is done under the watchful eye of the editor, who must clear all changes. These treatments of the piece ready it for typesetting so that layouts can be tightened and designed with the actual type. At some point, titles and subheads are discussed and decided on and quotes are pulled for design. The material takes on a graphic life of its own.

Work beyond this stage occurs internally and has to do with fitting the piece to the allotted space. Writers aren't ordinarily involved in these stages. With a heavily reported piece, I always want the writer to be involved in the cutting because cutting can create inaccuracies and the writer knows his material best. Once a piece has been "shipped," the writer should lean back and wait to get a check and see his article in print.

□ **What endears writers to you?**
Willingness to take chances, but also to be talked down from the ledge. Sometimes writers get stuck. Editors can help if writers will let them.

Attention to detail and craft.

Treating editors with courtesy and consideration.

Respecting deadlines.

And length. If the editor asks for 1,000 words and a writer hands in 1250, that's not too bad. More than that, forget it. It's not just a matter of too many words. The editor considers it no favor if she has asked for 1,000 words and the article has 3,000. It's not just a matter of cutting. That piece is an entirely different genre and must be rewritten, not cut. When writers go over, they're not in control of their material. On the other hand, if the editor asks for 1,000 words and the writer hands in 750—that's not good either. The editor is trying to fill a slot. And, once again, it's a different kind of piece at that shorter length.

□ **Why is publishing so difficult today—for writers in search of magazines in which to be published and for editors in search of good writers?**
Magazine publishing and book publishing are no longer white-glove businesses.

They aren't the incubators of literary talent that they once were. Editors are under a lot of pressure today. It costs money to take a gamble on a new writer, only to have him or her turn in unacceptable work. That reflects badly on the editor, who is expected to know whether an assigned article will work out. That's why good writers are in high demand and unproven writers have a hard time breaking in.

□ What do you advise writers who need to develop their writing skills in order to be published?

Be the guardian of *your* craft, writing.

The desire in people to write is so strong that it can actually carry them to areas where their skills aren't that terrific. If they are honest about what they're not great at and apply themselves, they can surprise themselves and surpass their own expectations. Basically, writers must be good at absorbing and conveying information. Here's what they can do:

Practice digesting newspaper and magazine pieces. If a piece is 500 words, rewrite it to 250. Ask a partner if you did a decent job and to tell you what you missed. Don't balk. A pattern will develop. Attack your weaknesses with more practice. Learn to understand your strengths.

To understand structure, analyze pieces that you like. What percentage of the piece is devoted to quotes, straight information, and the writer's own point of view? Break pieces down into their various components and see how they work. Magazine articles are like little watch works. Compare pieces from different publications treating the same subject. Then you'll begin to differentiate among magazines, too.

Pull magazine pieces that you like and make a file—short, long, and in-between. Analyze length. Be completely familiar with what a 1,000-word piece is. Count every word, read the piece, and understand how it began, developed, and ended. Do the same with 3,000- and 500-word articles. When pitching a piece, you will be able to say with confidence, "Five hundred words will be perfect because I know what five hundred words is."

Lastly, read newspapers, magazines, nonfiction books, stories, poems, and novels with an attention to style. Prime that pump, in effect.

□ Do you have other words of wisdom to freelance writers who want a future in magazine publishing?

Start small. Query editors on subjects that you know backwards and forwards and that you definitely can handle.

Spread yourself around. Have several queries out for different types of articles. (I'm not talking about multiple submissions).

Accumulate clips.

Find a few special editors with whom you can build a future, who will ultimately help you grow.

□ **What is your basic advice to writers?**

Do the best work you can, concern yourself with craft, and pay attention to detail. If you're good enough, editors will have to use you. Editors cannot do their jobs without writers. It's that simple.

4

Writing for Today's Magazines

LESLIE LAND, SENIOR EDITOR

Yankee
Dublin, New Hampshire

LESLIE LAND majored in political science in college. After graduation, she worked as a chef at an upscale gourmet restaurant. She began to write about food and gardening and worked as a freelance writer until 1989, when she became the contributing editor for gardening for *Metropolitan Home*. Land then took on the food position at *House & Garden* and from there went to *First for Women*, a mass-market super market women's magazine with a circulation of about 1.5 million, where her duties became entirely editorial. Land is now the senior editor for food and home at *Yankee* magazine. "I do food, gardening, collecting, home renovations, anything to do with home life—you name it," says Land.

"*Yankee* is a true general-interest magazine," adds Land. "Literature, travel, journalism, services—if it's New England, we cover it." Founded in 1935 by Robb Sagendorph, *Yankee* is a monthly regional magazine with a national audience. Its circulation is 700,000.

☐ **How are magazines similar or different editorially?**
Each magazine is the sum of its editors. The mix of editors differs from one publication to another. Some love to discover new talent while others are constitutionally disposed against it.

☐ **How can freelance writers break in?**
Freelancers who are skilled at writing snappy query letters are more likely to make it into the process than those who may be perfectly good writers but don't want to spend the time writing queries or do not have the gift of compression.

□ What do you mean by the "gift of compression"?

The shorter the query you can hook me with, the likelier I am to be interested. A stranger pitching a story will have about twenty seconds of my attention. I will read or skim the first paragraph. I'll either see something that interests me or not.

□ Do you therefore urge writers to work on their query-writing skills?

Yes, if they want to break in where they are strangers.

□ What tips would you give writers about a good query letter?

Make it easy to read. If you're still working with a typewriter, use a clean ribbon. If a proposal is difficult to read, it may not get read. The same holds true for content—be clear and concise. Send clips. Unless the story idea is so fabulous that I am lying on the floor panting, I'm not going to call the writer and ask for clips.

□ How are editorial decisions made?

That depends entirely on the structure of a given magazine. Certain magazines make decisions entirely from the top down—even senior editors don't have the final say. Other magazines are more collegial. Every magazine looks for balance. If we run a difficult story, a long story, or a sad story, we're going to want to run another story that is accessible, short, or upbeat to keep a good mix.

□ What do editors want from writers?

To start, a good article. It's just like any job. You are more likely to get work if you turn assignments in on time and at a proper length, and if you work well with the editor. Editors love writers who recognize problems and deal with them efficiently. If the person you're writing about dies, you'd better tell the editor. And when you do, have an idea about how to keep the story itself alive.

□ Is it helpful for a writer to retain an agent?

There are a few magazines where it is marginally easier to get in if you have an agent, assuming that the agent is well connected there, but there aren't many. Most magazines don't pay well enough to interest agents anyway. Don't forget, they're only making 15 percent on the deal.

□ What are your pet peeves?

Phone calls. Don't *think* about calling an editor. A phone query is a waste of time until the author is sufficiently in with that editor.

Heavily edited clips. A writer sends me a bunch of good clips. I commission a story. Then I discover that what's good is all of the previous editors that this writer has had.

Writers who ignore assignment instructions. If I have commissioned you to give me a 1,200- to 1,500-word story by X and you give me 3,500 words two weeks later than X, I'm going to be very unhappy.

□ **What do you advise writers who want to be published in magazines?**
It's like giving people advice on how to eat a healthful diet. In spite of all of the embroidery and the latest developments, the rules have been the same for one hundred years. Eat more fruits and vegetables, less grease and meat. Advice on getting published? Write well. Speak clearly. Keep it short. If you're just starting out, turn down nothing. You need clips, you need credits, you need published examples of work you're proud of.

In order to earn a living as a freelance writer, you must be able to write fast and consistently. Magazines do not pay well. If you can't crank it out, you're going to starve.

□ **What is your opinion of magazines as sources of work for writers in this country today?**
It's low. Increasingly, authors don't write articles for magazines; they write captions. Many magazines are primarily interested in the writer's connections, sources, and story ideas, since editors can rewrite anything. Freelancers often have the deflating experience of seeing their best material whacked and hacked to smithereens. You've got to be able to shrug that off and keep going.

5

Commonsense Ideas: What Every Writer Should Know and Do

FRAN CARPENTIER, SENIOR EDITOR
PARADE
New York

FRAN CARPENTIER was a journalism major in college. After graduation, she worked for a short time in book publishing before moving to magazines. Carpentier helped start a women's service magazine called *Be Alive*. After the publication folded, she became managing editor of *Lady's Circle*. Carpentier was promoted to editor in chief within six months. "That's where I cut my [publishing] teeth," says Carpentier. "But you [shouldn't] be editor in chief of anything at twenty-four years old." In 1979 she went to *Parade*, where she worked her way up from associate editor to senior editor.

Founded in the early 1940s, *Parade* is published weekly as a magazine supplement of major Sunday newspapers. "*Parade* does not replace or compete with the newspapers in which we're distributed," explains Carpentier. "To add our own voice, we give our readers stories that they won't see elsewhere." *Parade* is distributed to 37.1 million homes. "We have 81 million readers," says Carpentier. "It's really daunting, isn't it?"

□ **What must a writer do to be published in major magazines like *Parade*?**
A writer must focus an idea so that the story will appeal to most readers. We want the most compelling angle.

☐ **Tell me about a typical *Parade* story that had a compelling angle. How was it acquired?**

Several years ago I received a query from a freelancer who wanted to write a story about guns. She called to discuss the proposal. Initially, I thought, "There is no way that a 1,500- to 1,800-word *Parade* article can resolve whether Americans should have the right to bear arms." But during our conversation the writer explained that she was a single mother living in a Los Angeles neighborhood that was getting dangerous. Although she had been a New York City liberal, raised in the lap of luxury, she was now thinking of getting a license and buying a gun to protect herself and her son. That became a totally different story, a fascinating essay of one young single mother's view of the dangers she and her son were facing. Our discussion led to an assignment, which eventually became a cover story titled "Why I Own a Gun." I would challenge any reader to turn away from that story, no matter how he or she feels about guns. When you see that headline, and that point of view, it's hard *not* to read the story.

☐ **What is the basic purpose of a query?**

A query should show an editor how a writer thinks and should initiate a dialogue between the writer and the editor. The brass ring on the end of the query is an assignment. But that's not always going to happen. Nevertheless, it will demonstrate the writer's skill and show the editor what he might depend on the writer for.

☐ **Will a well-written query help a writer create a successful article?**

Yes. The piece should flow from a well-structured query. The writer must put almost as much work into the query as he or she would put into the article. At the very least, a writer should be accurate in terms of promising what can actually be delivered.

☐ **Should writers create a title for the piece in the query?**

If you've got a fabulous title, by all means use it. Creating titles is a real skill. A query came to my desk for a story called "The Value of Teaching Teenagers Cardiopulmonary Resuscitation." I bet you're already asleep [from that title], aren't you? We called it "Kids Who Save Lives." Our title was punchier, more compelling.

☐ **How can writers create titles?**

I could say, make the title sexier, but I don't mean that the writer should cheapen the story or make it hysterical or silly. The writer must think more like an editor—what is the most compelling aspect of the story?

☐ **Why do some talented writers get repeated rejections?**

Because they submit ideas for stories that they want to write, which the vast majority of people don't want to read.

□ **What do editors want from writers in addition to good ideas and good writing?**

Editors want writers to be reliable and trustworthy. Accuracy is essential, especially at *Parade*, because we have the ability to influence public opinion and we're always very mindful of our responsibility to our readers. That's got to come first. If a writer says that 20 percent of the American people suffer from an ailment, the editor must feel certain that it's 20 percent and not 2 percent. Editors must be confident that writers will get all the right information and that they will listen to the editor, do their homework, and deliver on time.

□ **Why is it difficult for new writers to be published in magazines like** *Parade?*

Writing is a business. We have 81 million readers. That's a tremendous opportunity for any writer. On the flip side, we have a tremendous responsibility to give our readers the best story possible. The bottom line is—and this is a harsh reality—we're going to give assignments to writers who are used to navigating their way through labyrinthine paths. If you were the editor of a large national magazine and you had to give someone an assignment to cover the hottest celebrity of the moment, who would you go to? You'd go to a writer who knows your style and policies, who will do the best job, and who will deliver.

□ **If writers study your magazine carefully, can they figure out how to entice you?**

I think they can, but I say that with reservation. *Parade* is always a good read. Some people might infer that *Parade* is an easy market and therefore think, "I could write these stories with my eyes closed." I challenge any writer to try. My editor in chief often reminds us: "If a story reads easy, it wrote hard, and if it reads hard, it wrote easy." It's not unusual for writers, even leading, well-known writers, to have to go through several revisions before a piece is accepted. Also, at *Parade* we do not plan our lineup according to a formula. It's not easy to plug into *Parade*.

□ **Can writers learn to turn news into feature stories?**

I'm not so sure. In theory, if they read the books that explain what editors really want, they should be more successful at selling their stories to a variety of publications. But are they *really* going to get it? The truth is, as in any industry, maybe only 5 percent are going to make it. Trying to become a better writer is like trying to diet successfully. You often stick to the way you've been doing things.

□ **What major mistakes do freelance writers make?**

Many writers work hard, but they don't work smart. They conduct their business in a gunshot style, sending the same ideas to many editors. They don't focus a topic specifically to one magazine.

Writers try to create lead sentences that will grab the editor. But the leads are often amateurish. I received one from a writer who was obviously trying to get my attention. It read, "Have you ever woken up in the morning wanting to slap your mother in the face?" That was not a compelling sentence. It was off-putting.

Also, a week after we have published an article, we often receive a slew of almost identical ideas. The writer's logic—"I know you do this kind of story." But we just published that story. This happens all the time.

□ Do top writers make mistakes?

Yes. Big-name writers who have been in the writing business for a long time sometimes fail to focus their idea, assuming that their reputation is enough to sell it. At *Parade*, that's not so. Everyone must do his homework.

A senior editor at another magazine, who participated on writers panels where he offered advice to freelancers, wanted to write for *Parade*. So he submitted the names of three celebrities, two of whom were known only to New York audiences. That was his first sin. Then, he did not explain why he was qualified to write these profiles. And he did not give me any idea of his angle, his approach to the story, or how he hoped to elicit who these celebrities really were—what made them tick and so on. I was stunned—and disappointed—by his cavalier approach. Needless to say, he did not get an assignment.

□ What advice would you give writers?

When pitching ideas, tell the story straight. Don't pitch your story in "gee whiz" fashion ("Wow! Isn't Liam Neeson the greatest star?"). At the same time, don't pitch the idea as though you are larger than your idea—the haughty approach.

Don't come with an ax to grind. Writers who bring their own point of view into a story are looking for trouble. I've told writers, "You have an interesting point of view, but the way you're proposing it belongs on the op-ed page of the *New York Times*. If you're writing for *Parade*, we want a balanced view."

Think of yourself as successful. That's the image you want to present. In the end, it will help you put together a better story because you will earn the regard and respect of the people you are interviewing and the people from whom you are trying to get information. Never sell yourself short. We're all much smarter than we give ourselves credit for.

6

What Ifs

What If a Writer Sends Multiple Queries? What If the Writer Doesn't Meet His or Her Deadline? What If the Submitted Article Isn't What the Writer and Editor Originally Agreed On? What If the Writer Doesn't Get Along with His or Her Editor? What If the Article Is Published, But the Freelancer Wasn't Paid? What If the Writer Is Paid, But the Article Wasn't Published? and More

BOB SULLIVAN, SENIOR EDITOR

Life
New York

BOB SULLIVAN holds an undergraduate degree in English and a master's degree in journalism. His first job after graduate school was assistant editor at a small New Hampshire magazine. In 1980 he joined *Sports Illustrated* as a reporter, where he climbed the ranks to become editor. In 1992 Sullivan helped start an Australian edition of *Sports Illustrated*. At the end of that year, he returned to the United States to join *Life* magazine as senior editor. Sullivan is in charge of *Life*'s "Face-to-Face" section.

Life magazine was founded in 1936. The famous weekly *Life* magazine folded in 1972. When it closed, its circulation was over 10 million. "It became a question of postal rates, subscription increases, and so on," says Sullivan. "Rather than cut the rate base, they folded what was one of the biggest magazines in the country." The monthly *Life* magazine was brought back in 1982. According to Sullivan, the new *Life* has grown and thrived. *Life*'s present circulation is over 2 million.

□ **Does *Life* accept freelance contributions?**
Rarely. Ninety-five to 98 percent of the magazine is staff-written.

□ **Who writes the other 3 to 5 percent?**
Freelance writers who have special access to difficult-to-access people, like Ted Turner, for example, who is famously reclusive. However, we won't do the article unless Ted also agrees to the story *and* lets us go to the ranch to photograph him and Jane on the horses.

If access implies that the writer wants to do only a positive profile of a person, he's wasting his time. We don't do puff pieces. We don't do negative stories, either.

□ **How much do you pay?**
We pay $4,000 for a "Face-to-Face" feature of about 2,500 to 3,000 words.

□ **Let's talk about "what ifs." What if a writer doesn't direct the query to a named editor?**
If the query is sent to "The Editor," it will get lost.

□ **What if a writer doesn't use letterhead stationery?**
That's okay if he or she sets up a [computer] letterhead with the address on top in a formal letter format. The writer doesn't have to have his or her own stationery. It could be a question of finances. We know that freelancing is tough.

□ **What if the query has typos?**
I would think negatively about that. That is unprofessional.

□ **What if the writer neglects to enclose a self-addressed, stamped envelope with his query?**
We probably won't respond if our reply is negative.

□ **What if the writer calls the editor about a query?**
A phone call is perfectly fine if an editor has shirked his responsibility and not responded to the writer in an expedient fashion.

□ **What if a writer sends multiple queries and more than one magazine offers an assignment?**
Writers should not submit multiple queries. That writer is not in an enviable position. He's in a pickle. Multiple queries are not professional.

□ **Who is responsible for communication between the editor and the writer after a piece is assigned?**
The editor is primarily responsible. The editor should give the direction and warnings, too.

□ **What if a writer is assigned an article at a magazine and doesn't get along with his editor?**
That can happen. But writers must understand magazines and magazine editors. The job of the magazine's top editor is to serve his readership. That's the charge he hands down to all his editors. If the editor suggests a change, the writer must bear in mind that the editor's job is to think about the readership.

Magazines have subscribers. Magazine editors must think of their subscriber base and what people expect of the magazine. The edit has to be tailored to the readership. If an editor tells you something that conflicts with what you as an individual writer feel, and this happens a lot, it's a problem that you're going to have to accept. You must be willing to accept suggestions and changes or magazine writing will be a constant source of frustration to you.

If you're always going to feel that your story deserves three thousand words when the assignment was two thousand words, you'll have botched the assignment by delivering three thousand words. This is where most conflicts come up. Writers say, "I'm not getting enough space. I'm not getting my point across." Magazines do not depend on their writers; they depend on their readers. Since editors are trying to serve that readership, it's sometimes difficult to serve writers as well. I ask a writer to think about why he or she is having this difficulty. If it has to do with misinterpreting what is expected of him, he should have a philosophical talk with himself and try to redirect his attention toward the readership. If the problem lies with the writer, the writer can deal with it himself.

□ **What if the problem *is* the editor?**
If an editor is sheepish in dealing with his managing editor or isn't giving the writer an opinion or isn't giving good direction, the problem is a faulty editor. That's much more difficult for the writer to deal with. This is a very unfortunate circumstance for the freelance writer and a very difficult one to extricate himself from. The writer can pull his piece back, terminate his contract, and try to negotiate the kill fee. Or he could swallow his pride, let the piece go, and let the editor do what he will.

□ Is it possible for a freelance writer to change editors?

It is possible if you have a good relationship with the magazine. But if you don't know the magazine, you're asking for somebody who you presume will be better, but you don't know.

□ Will the writer who refuses to make changes get paid by allowing the editor to revise the article?

Yes, that writer will receive a full fee. But the writer who won't allow revisions and refuses to let the magazine publish the piece won't. Magazines don't exist as a forum for the writer's opinions. They're here to serve the readers. That writer will get a kill fee because it's in the contract. The magazine has trusted that the assignment will work out; if it doesn't, the kill fee is the magazine's good faith guarantee. The writer is then free to sell the article elsewhere. If the article was never published and the writer received full payment, it can still be sold to another magazine if it's legally returned to the writer.

□ What if the submitted article isn't what the writer and editor originally agreed on in terms of length, angle, or subject?

If the editor did his or her job, it will be headed toward a kill fee. If that editor spelled out to the writer in no uncertain terms the length, subject matter, and reporting, and the writer didn't cooperate, the story is doomed.

□ Tell me about problems with length.

Even with our staffers, if a piece is supposed to run 3,000 words and the writer has 4,000 words of gem-like prose, I'll look at it and we can talk. But it's not going to run at 4,000 words. If the writer hands in 3,100 words that he has chiseled down and it's very good, he'll likely be pleased with the piece. If the writer hands in 4,500 words and says, "You cut the next 1,500, I just can't get another word out of here," the readership may still be just as pleased, but the writer will inevitably be unhappy.

One of the adages in journalism is it's much easier to write a 10,000-word piece than a 5,000-word piece. If the assignment is 5,000 words, you do a lot of reporting. And you want to spill it all out. It's easier to write that longer draft. The tough part is to chisel the piece into something good and leave some of words you have fallen in love with on the cutting room floor. It's hard to part with these words.

□ What if the writer doesn't meet his deadline?

Blowing a deadline is inexcusable and it's unprofessional to miss the deadline without telling your editor. It's usually clear to any writer several days in advance if he's going to miss his deadline. He should call the editor and ask if that will create problems. I often say, "That's fine," because we work well ahead. I say, "If you're really struggling, I understand; take another week."

Calling an editor four days in advance and asking for another three days is not blowing a deadline. That's adjusting a deadline. Adjusting a deadline is a perfectly fine practice if it's okay with the editor. However, if the editor says, "No, we've got your piece in the current issue and our production schedule just can't handle that," you have to do the article. You stay up all night and get it into as good a shape as you can. The deadline is the contract.

□ **Is a writer's bad attitude the kiss of death for future assignments at that magazine?**
If the writer demands that the magazine publish the piece without edits? Oh yes, that's it! Why would an editor go back to that writer and take a chance that it might happen again?

□ **Will there be an industry-wide stigma against that writer?**
Absolutely not. We don't compare notes. A writer with such a firm opinion about the article may find another magazine that agrees with his or her opinion. Eventually this strong-minded writer may find a proper home.

□ **What do you advise freelance writers who want to be published in major magazines?**
Be realistic. Be professional. Understand both sides of the business. Editors have jobs to do, only part of which is dealing with freelancers and freelance submissions. You can't expect an editor to deal with your query [as soon as he receives it]. That's unrealistic.

Magazine writing is a great profession. I encourage freelancers to broaden their interests. The wonderful thing about writing magazine articles is the breadth of education you can afford yourself by dealing with various subjects. The way to stay stimulated is to make the assignment you choose interesting. Then you'll do the best job.

Be willing to start small. Everybody wants to get published in all of the biggies right away. Getting published in smaller magazines is a great way to hone your craft. They are rungs on the ladder. Climb the rungs and ultimately you can be published in *The New Yorker* and *The Atlantic* and *Sports Illustrated*. Those rungs are attainable, but you usually can't jump over the other rungs to get to them.

7

The Evolution of Women's Magazines

JUDITH DANIELS, EXECUTIVE EDITOR
Self
Former Contributing Editor at Glamour
Founder of Savvy
New York

JUDITH DANIELS graduated from Smith College with honors in English. She went to New York to work in book publishing, but "accidentally" switched to magazines when she heard about a job at a new weekly called *New York* magazine. "It sounded like a perfectly terrible job, sort of low man in the art department in charge of not losing photographs," says Daniels. "I took the job anyway. If I didn't like it, I told them, I was going to quit in two weeks." She stayed for eight years.

Daniels fell in love with magazine publishing. After keeping an eye on the photographs at *New York* for a few months, Daniels started editing manuscripts, developing story ideas, and assigning column and feature articles. She rapidly climbed the ranks from editor to managing editor. When *The Village Voice* was acquired by New York Magazine Company, Daniels was asked to be managing editor there. When she left the company, it was to launch her own publication, *Savvy*, a magazine for executive and professional women. Four years later she went to Time Inc., where she worked on *Money* and *People* and was the editor of *Life* for two years. At the time of this interview Daniels was contributing editor at *Glamour* and a publishing consultant. *Glamour* was founded in 1939. Its monthly circulation is about 2.3 million. Daniels is now the executive editor of *Self* magazine.

□ The emergence of the new working woman

In the mid-1970s, Daniels began to sense changes for women. She observed a new kind of working woman. "There was a great excitement and self-consciousness about our jobs," Daniels explains, "a headiness as more and more women uncovered their talents and took on management and leadership roles. The sexiest thing was good shoptalk."

There was no magazine that spoke to upper-echelon working women about their personal lives, their work lives, and their political lives. Magazines on the newsstands addressed women as "full-time homemakers, full-time clotheshorses, or full-time very embattled feminists." (At that time *Working Woman* was more downmarket than it eventually became.) "What the world needed was a magazine that integrated work, self, and society for the emerging community of higher-education, higher-job level, higher-income women," says Daniels.

□ The founding of *Savvy*

Daniels worked up 150 story ideas to convince herself that this idea had staying power. She went to circulation and advertising experts to help determine whether such a magazine had promise. "Every woman I talked to understood what I was saying and every man I talked to said, 'There are plenty of women's magazines out there. What do you need another women's magazine for?'" says Daniels.

Clay Felker, founder of *New York* and now head of the Felker Magazine Center at UC–Berkeley, invited Daniels to preview her new magazine in *New York* (just as he had previewed *Ms.* for Gloria Steinem in 1970). The positive response to the *New York* preview encouraged Daniels to continue with the entrepreneurial challenge: finding investors and financing, conducting direct mail tests, and revising countless business plans. It took two years, but the first issue of *Savvy* was launched in January 1980.

□ How did you settle on the name *Savvy*?

We were working on this special issue of *New York* and I hadn't yet named my magazine. I was considering *Achieve, Advance, Ahead, Aspire,* but they all began to sound like federally funded programs for the disadvantaged. Instead, I baptized it *Savvy.*

□ How did *Savvy* differ from *Ms.*?

I'm sure *Ms.* considered us very elitist. Indeed, *Savvy* was for women who had achieved some success on the job—or who aspired to it. But I always thought of *Savvy* as a magazine for mainstream feminists—women who were aware of the discriminatory and challenging problems in their world and wanted to do something about them. I don't think *Savvy* could have happened without the women's movement and *Ms.* On the other hand, *Ms.* left out certain important constituencies, and that made it possible for *Savvy* to strike a chord—with readers and advertisers.

□ How does *Glamour* fit into the spectrum?

The modern *Glamour* started over twenty years ago with Ruth Whitney, the current editor in chief. *Glamour* is a premier fashion and beauty magazine as well as a solidly journalistic publication, winning prizes for its social and political coverage. It's a full-service magazine encompassing travel, food, careers, personal finance, health—lots of health—and all manner of relationships. *Glamour* is the one of its type of magazine with an editorial page. It is unabashedly feminist and pro-choice, but it is willing to give plenty of voice to readers and writers who take other positions, too.

⊔ Why are there so many women's lifestyle magazines?

Women do not compartmentalize their lives and they do not need their source of information to be totally separate. They are accustomed to seeing—they *like* to see—their whole life reflected in their publications. There's no cognitive dissonance in reading investigative and political stories right next to celebrity, beauty, and fashion coverage. The total package—the intense mix of entertainment, education, fantasy, and values—validates a life.

□ What about men's magazines? Aren't *GQ* and *Esquire* about lifestyle?

We think of men buying single-focus publications—boating, cars, woodworking, computers, and so on. Men have not traditionally been comfortable with a lifestyle environment and are only now in relatively small circulation publications getting the mix of material that defines women's magazines. Those fashion-consuming, health-conscious, sexually anxious, fiction-reading, sensitive fathers are a relatively recent phenomenon.

□ How do women's magazines differ from each other, and what does this mean to freelance writers?

To people on the outside, women's magazines are pretty monolithic, but as you get closer to them, you see very different goals, age targets, sensibilities, and modes of execution—how different editors speak to the audience that they are selling to advertisers.

Freelancers must become students of magazines and not assume all women's magazines are alike. A writer's subject area—careers, personal finance, travel—may suit several publications, but the point of view, the level of sophistication, the tone of voice all change from one magazine to another. One may be a primer, while another assumes its readers are up to speed on the background, vocabulary, or technicality of a subject. Pay attention to the demographics. You can really turn off an editor with a query if you don't get something as basic as age and sophistication level right. And whatever you do, don't presume the lowest common denominator and be patronizing just because the magazine has millions of readers.

□ **How do magazine viewpoints differ? Give me an example of a story that you edited for** *Glamour.*

Because monthlies are not in the business of breaking hot news, they have to get close to a subject from the reader's point of view. At *Glamour*, we can take a large topic in the news and zero in on a small slice of it, or we can take a single, much-covered event and add other examples from a constituency for an overview.

At *Glamour* recently the editors were very touched by a manuscript from a woman whose son had died of AIDS, but because *Glamour* is so focused on women in their twenties and thirties, the mother's story, no matter how affecting, was wrong for us. Fortunately, the author had the skill and strength to rewrite the piece, focusing on the young women who loved her son. Our readers identified with the drama of pain and love and caring.

Another example: Historian Patricia O'Toole waded into a swamp of spreading homophobia, racism, and anti-Semitism in Cobb County, Georgia. There she found three young women who had never been politically active before but who took a stand, saying no to hate and prejudice. Cobb County had certainly been in the headlines and editorials around the country, but our readers felt the issues to the core when they saw how those issues affected women like them.

□ **Do top women's magazines deal with agents?**

Agents are not a necessary entry for the beginning writer, and most agents don't like to bother with short magazine articles anyway.

□ **Do you prefer to work with an expert in a specific field or an experienced journalist?**

Glamour is always interested in identifying the expert with fresh insights, ideas, and data, but we find that an experienced journalist is generally more successful than the M.D. or the Ph.D. in interpreting such material for our readers.

□ **Why are women's magazines a good market for freelance writers?**

Women's magazines are a great showcase. These publications are read by millions, and as a writer, you have a chance to effect change.

□ **What changes have you seen in women's magazines?**

Women's magazines today are smarter, more varied, wider-reaching, more political, more daring than they have ever been. (Indeed, women's magazines are winning prizes for their reporting, even beating out the news weeklies.) They are more respectful of the reader's challenges and choices. Thanks to their magazines, women have become very tough consumers and demand ever tougher information from what they read. All magazines are up against a lot of competition for readers' time—television, other media, and women's own complicated work and family demands. Magazines are forced to be better at entertaining, informing, and holding the reader's attention.

□ Will women's magazines change in the future?

Women's magazines are both extremely durable and very responsive. As the baby boom women age, the next big opportunity will be the kind of magazine that no one has been able to get right in the past: a comprehensive, lively publication for older women.

8

The Evolution of Men's Magazines

EDWARD KOSNER, EDITOR IN CHIEF
Esquire
New York

EDWARD KOSNER majored in English and history in college. After graduation, he worked as a rewrite man and editor at the *New York Post*. He joined *Newsweek* in 1963, and worked there as a writer and editor for sixteen years, serving as editor of the magazine from 1975 to 1979. Kosner became editor of *New York* magazine in 1980, rose to publisher in 1986, and was promoted to editor and president in 1991. He has been editor in chief of *Esquire* since October 1993.

Esquire was founded in 1933 and has maintained its original mixture of service material and fashion coverage for men. Over the years *Esquire* has published articles by many important writers, including Ernest Hemingway, F. Scott Fitzgerald, Gay Talese, Julie Baumgold, and Tom Wolfe.

Esquire's monthly circulation is about 750,000. The audience is 70 percent men and 30 percent women.

□ **What purpose did *Esquire* originally serve and how has it evolved? How does it compare to the competition?**
Esquire was designed to be exactly what it is today—an ambitious magazine of journalism, literary material, and service to entertain and inform men. GQ started out as a fashion magazine and evolved into a magazine of fashion and general articles. *Playboy*, the incarnation of Hugh Hefner's vision, was built initially around nude centerfolds. The articles and short stories came later and evolved to compete with the explicit material.

□ **How do you categorize *Esquire*? How does it differ from GQ, its primary competition?**

Esquire is a topical magazine of journalism for men with a literary flair, a sense of humor, and important service elements. *Esquire* is an articles magazine with fashion. GQ is a fashion magazine with articles.

□ **Who reads *Esquire*? What does it offer readers?**

The median age of our readers is the mid-thirties, ranging from college age to people in their fifties and sixties. We try to balance material so that at least two or three pieces in each issue will appeal to different parts of our core readership. That's known in the trade as "the mix."

We publish articles that are timely—not necessarily breaking news, but events and interests of the time—on subjects that haven't already been covered.

□ **How do magazines like *Esquire* and GQ differ from comparable women's magazines?**

I don't think there is a female equivalent of *Esquire*, unless you think of *Vanity Fair* as a women's magazine, which it fundamentally is in terms of readership and advertising. Of the women's magazines, *Glamour* may come closest, but it doesn't run topical journalism the way *Esquire* does. GQ [might be] the men's equivalent of *Vogue*.

□ **Many articles in *Esquire* are interesting to women. Why isn't it considered a magazine for men and women?**

Part of the hope is that interested women *will* read the magazine. *Esquire* has always had a loyal group of women readers, women writers, and women editors. But it is fundamentally a men's magazine. I would not choose an article for *Esquire* that women would read and that men wouldn't. But I would choose an article that men would read and women wouldn't. Ideally, I wouldn't have to make that choice.

□ **How do men's magazines such as *Esquire* differ from general-interest magazines?**

Esquire is closer to a general-interest magazine than most of the other men's magazines. I am basically a general-interest magazine editor.

□ **Why would someone pick up *Esquire* rather than *Atlantic* magazine, *Vanity Fair*, or *People*?**

The answer is, if the articles look interesting, they'll pick it up. If the articles are not interesting, they won't. These magazines all deal with contemporary life and contemporary culture, some with a more intellectual or cerebral or literary take and some with a more pop tabloid take.

□ Give me an example of a typical *Esquire* article.

It's hard to say what a typical article is because they are very eclectic. I'm looking at one issue that has an interview with Woody Allen, in which he talks about the trials and tribulations of his life; a piece by Jimmy Breslin called "Jealousy, Rage, Murder and Other Acts of Love," about violent male jealousy; and a profile of Don Imus, the radio personality.

□ How do you usually acquire articles?

Most of the articles are written by staff writers or people who are on contract to us. An occasional freelance writer will contribute one piece a year.

□ What is required for a successful *Esquire* article?

The trick is to combine the subject, the writer, and the timing. That combination makes a very successful article.

□ Are all queries read at *Esquire*?

I read all the queries. If one has potential, I pass it on to an articles editor to scrutinize. Many are disqualified simply because the subject has been done or it's obvious from the query or writing samples that the person can't write at the level of polish and sophistication that we need. Or because we're already working on the story. Or because it's too obscure. Many people send us reminiscence pieces—"I grew up with Keith Richards. I have a great idea for a piece on Keith Richards' early years." Unless the writer is Brendan Behan, we wouldn't want it.

□ Why is it so difficult for a new writer to break in at *Esquire*?

Because we only publish about sixty articles a year and we have our pick of writers. We can get Mailer, Breslin, Gary Wills—practically anybody. We also work with writers who aren't familiar to the larger public, but are known within the magazine world. They have credentials. They've written articles for important magazines. We know their work. For every Jimmy Breslin and Norman Mailer, there are many very fine journalists whose names are not household phrases.

□ How can a first-time writer break in?

He or she must have unique material and be able to write. The article must be equivalent to a "60 Minutes" story—something compelling that I haven't heard about. A decent writer who has unique access to an especially compelling story will also have a chance to break in.

□ Give me an example of a first-time writer who broke in at *Esquire*?

There was a group of young, Generation X people called Crusties because they didn't bathe very often. They are like modern hoboes who ride around the country on freight cars and live off the land. Some are fairly comfortable but have chosen this life—there may be a drug coefficient to it.

A young writer who traveled with them wrote a very compelling piece. She offered access to a world that no one knew existed and certainly no one else had been in. It didn't matter what her previous writing credentials were. She wrote the piece adequately. In that case, she offered reporting. That's more valuable than the 114 essays that I get saying, "The slacker generation is misunderstood." We aren't looking for self-expression from young, untried writers. We are looking for reporting.

It wasn't the brilliance of her prose or the sensitivity of her psyche. She went out and got a story that nobody else had gotten. That's the best single way to break in.

□ Do you have other advice for writers?

Don't spell the editor's name wrong.

Don't make grammatical errors in your query letter.

Don't query on articles that have already appeared in the magazine.

You're not likely to get anywhere with personal thoughts and essays—what we call "wall writing," where you turn your face to the wall and gaze at it for inspiration.

Magazines like *Esquire* look for reporting on subjects that have real appeal. The obscure, offbeat piece is almost certain not to be picked up.

9

Author-Editor Etiquette

LYNN POVICH, EDITOR IN CHIEF
Working Woman
New York

LYNN POVICH majored in modern European history and minored in French and English in college. After graduation, she worked for a year and a half as a secretary/researcher at the *Newsweek* bureau in Paris. She returned to *Newsweek* in New York, where she stayed for twenty-five years, climbing the ranks from researcher to senior editor. In 1968 Povich was *Newsweek's* only female writer. When she was promoted to senior editor in 1975, she was the first woman to attain that position. In 1991 Povich joined *Working Woman* as editor in chief.

Working Woman was founded in 1976 as a mentor magazine for career-oriented women in their twenties. When Povich became editor in chief, the readers' average age was thirty-eight and they were in executive and management positions or business owners. *Working Woman's* monthly circulation is 750,000.

☐ **How do you categorize *Working Woman*?**
Working Woman is the only national women's business magazine—the information resource of and for business and professional women.

☐ **What's the competition?**
Interestingly enough, there is no competition. There is no other magazine that deals with women as professionals. The other women's magazines may have a page on careers; other business publications, such as *Business Week*, *Forbes*, and *Fortune*, are directed toward a predominantly male audience.

□ Why do professional and business women need their own business magazine?

Women want a broader-based business magazine because their approach is people-oriented. They will read the hard data that they need to know, but [they want more]. A woman's sense of business is the workplace—relationships with colleagues, bosses, and subordinates, pay equity, family, and career and management issues. They don't usually get that other information in business magazines.

□ Give me examples of articles published in *Working Woman.*

We publish articles about women's management and communication styles. We cover pay and personal finance issues that are unique to women. We do an annual salary survey that looks at the wage gap between men and women in various occupations. Each year, we published the twenty-five hottest careers for women and list the top fifty women business owners. We cover stories on why women are leaving corporate America, women who make more money than their husbands and how that shifts the decision making and the power in relationships, and sexual harassment in the workplace.

□ What percentage of the articles in *Working Woman* are written by freelancers?

We work with a regular group of freelance writers who have business expertise or a track record as feature writers. They write 80 percent to 85 percent of our articles.

□ How do you usually acquire articles?

We suggest articles to our regular contributors and they offer ideas to us. That is our first line of acquisition.

□ How should new writers approach you?

Writers we have never worked with should put their ideas in writing and send five to eight clips of various kinds of stories—news, profiles, and features. It is also helpful but not necessary to direct a query to a named editor. Without a name, it will take longer to get to the right editor. The writer must also understand the magazine. Most problems occur because freelancers suggest ideas that are inappropriate or not at the [proper] level of sophistication. They either miss the sense of what we're about, the audience, or the tone. Our angle is always from the managerial-executive's or entrepreneur's point of view.

□ What sparks your interest in a query? What should the query include?

We want fresh ideas, a new take on an old situation, or a story about someone who has accomplished something extraordinary, someone from whom our readers can learn. Women are always looking for a better idea, a take-away idea that they can apply to their own lives, whether it's how to overcome a problem or turn something around.

I know it's not thought of as a great thing to do, but frankly, I prefer to see a whole piece and not just a proposal. I can tell a lot more. An entire piece will tell me if the writer can integrate information, if the article is right for the magazine, and if the writer can write. *Working Woman* articles require a great deal of expertise. Writers must be able to formulate a story that has very specific information. I can deal with an article submitted on spec if it's a smart idea and is well written, even if it's slightly off base. I can reformulate the piece. I can go back to the writer and suggest changes. I don't like to see queries that are not thoroughly proofread and contain typos and bad grammar or the names of editors incorrect or misspelled.

□ **Is it okay for writers to call an editor if they haven't heard about a submitted query or manuscript?**
Yes. I'd call a week or so after it was mailed to see if it was received. Then call the editor again in a couple weeks to check on the story. That's not bad etiquette. A writer who wants to be sure of a response should always include a self-addressed, stamped envelope.

□ **Is it a good idea for a writer to resubmit a story after it has been rejected?**
The writer will know whether that's a good idea from the editor's letter. Hopefully, the editor will explain why the query was not right and will either leave the door ajar, and say revise it, or will definitely shut the door.

□ **How do you feel about multiple submissions?**
Multiple submissions are not okay—but if it's done, the writer should be honest. Tell me up front that the query was submitted to another magazine so I'll know what I'm up against.

□ **Is it a black mark against the writer if the query is accepted by more than one magazine?**
Not forever. If the writer and the idea are really good, I would say, "If you're going to do this, I want to see it first. I don't want to have this situation again."

□ **What is proper etiquette for a beginning writer in negotiating a contract for an article? Can new writers ask for more than you offer?**
No. What we offer beginning writers is standard. Most editors will tell how much they pay beginning writers. The pay scale can rise once a writer becomes a

regular contributor. Regular writers know what the fees are. Whether you can negotiate depends on who you are. If you contribute on a regular basis, fees are usually standard. We pay between $1 and $1.50 per word.

□ Is it okay for a beginning writer to ask for expense money?

Beginning writers can ask for expense money, but they should give us an idea of how much that would be. Money for travel has to be negotiated up front and approved. I won't give expense money so that writers can take people out to lunch.

□ Who is responsible for the editor-author relationship?

The editor is ultimately responsible because he or she puts the magazine together and must be sure that everything's in on time and everybody is on track. Most editors keep track of their writers. Some writers are high maintenance and require a lot of talk while others just go off, do the article, and turn it in. It depends on personalities and work styles. Every editor and author I know have slightly different relationships.

□ How do you deal with writers?

I ask writers to call me before they begin writing to discuss their research and reporting. I would much rather that the writer has a clear idea before he or she begins writing because I'd rather not do revisions. Once writers have written a story, it is often difficult for them to rewrite it because they have committed what they thought the story was to paper. So rather than commit the wrong story or a story that's off the angle or a story that doesn't include something that I feel strongly about to paper, I'd rather have a discussion with my writers first. Then they can write and we'll talk about fixes, emphases, or cuts.

□ What about the writer who won't do revisions after the article is submitted?

That's not good because writers are commissioned by the magazine. The editor asks the writer to do an article that the magazine deems suitable. An editor wants to work with a writer who will make those three extra phone calls or fix what has to be fixed. If the writer won't do that, the editor will have to and she won't want to work with that writer again.

□ Can the writer get an extension on a deadline if there's a legitimate problem?

Of course. Serious reasons, a small delay, yes. It also depends on whether the story has to go and on how tightly run the magazine is in terms of deadlines. Missed deadlines can mean the difference between making and missing an issue.

□ **What are your pet peeves?**
Missed deadlines, writers who won't do serious research or reporting, writers who disregard the query, and writers who are picky about their contracts.

□ **What is your definition of a writer who is a professional?**
A writer who is professional formulates a complete query so the editor will have a real sense of the story. She will describe the idea, tell how she will handle it, explain what readers will take away from the story, and state why it would be perfect for the magazine. If we accept it, the writer goes off and reports it. A professional writer knows who to go to for information, understands what a deadline is and files on deadline, and has organized her checking material.

□ **How do you advise writers who want to be published in *Working Woman* or other major magazines?**
Understand the magazine. Even if your idea isn't right, there's nothing [as wonderful as] a query that shows that the writer knows what the magazine is about and how we do stories. We appreciate someone who has taken the time to read our stories. When a writer says, "I read your piece last August on women who make more than men and I see my story in that vein," I know this person is familiar with the magazine and is looking at that idea from our point of view. That's called customer service.

10

Author-Editor Etiquette:
A Second Opinion

SUSAN STRECKER, EDITOR IN CHIEF
Baby Talk
New York

SUSAN STRECKER majored in English and minored in French in college. She "bounced around" in a variety of jobs before landing her first publishing position as editor of *Executive Female* magazine. She became editor of *Baby Talk* in 1988.

Founded in 1935, *Baby Talk* is the oldest baby magazine in the country. It is a how-to, informational publication targeted to expectant and new mothers and is published ten times a year. Its circulation is 1.1 million. *Baby Talk* is distributed free in department stores and maternity shops or is available through paid subscription; it is not found on newsstands.

☐ **Are baby magazines a good market for freelance writers?**
We're a market, but not a terrific market. About 25 percent of the magazine is written by freelancers.

Most of our articles are by experts with experience writing on baby care and pregnancy. Freelancers usually write features about moms getting through the day, a problem and how it was conquered, or something scary that happened—heartfelt stories that speak to our audience.

We are in constant need of a fresh look at subjects that we repeat often. So we're always looking for new writers to cover these subjects from a new angle—a fresh angle for the readers as well as for ourselves, to keep our own creative juices flowing. For instance, we cover topics on pregnancy and babies up to age two.

After a reader's child gets older, she may stop reading our magazine. But the next new mom needs to know how to bathe her baby, what to do about a fever, what to do in the emergency room, and so on, so we do those stories again.

□ What do you look for in a query?

I look for a really well-honed, focused idea—presented well, of course. The query should look neat and be free of typos. My interpretation of typos is if writers are sloppy at this stage, are they going to be sloppy when I ask them to research something? Writers shouldn't use the oldest ribbon in the world. I shouldn't have to photocopy the query so I can read it, which actually happens quite often. Letterhead isn't important because it can be costly to buy and I sympathize with writers who are just starting out. I also like to see an enclosed SASE because it shows a novice who has done his or her homework. It's also important that the writer really knows what subjects are relevant to our readership. All of these points will spark my interest.

□ Are you offended if a query is not directed to a named editor?

I don't have a problem with that, partly because we're very small and a writer might not be able to tell from the masthead what each editor does.

□ What do you think about multiple submissions?

I don't like them. The writer should state in his or her letter that this is a multiple submission. We become annoyed when we call an author to make an assignment only to discover that it was a multiple submission. On the other hand, sometimes *we* make authors wait a long time. I'm a little torn.

□ Do you ever send personalized rejections with suggestions?

No. Beginning writers have asked us why we rejected their stories. Unfortunately, we can't take the time to send personal notes on the rejection letters.

There are a million reasons why we reject articles. We could have twelve in the hopper on the same subject, or we may have just done it, or the writer is just not right for the story.

□ Will you ever reconsider an article idea that you previously rejected?

If I said no to the idea once, I meant it.

□ Is it proper for a writer to try to negotiate the payment?

Not a first-time writer. The inexperienced writer has to accept what is offered. A writer who is building clips must bite the bullet, even if it turns out to be more work than he or she dreamed. After that, with more experience and more clips, the freelancer can try to edge the payment up.

□ Should writers ask for expense money?

Yes, especially if they are making phone calls all over the country.

□ **How does the author-editor relationship develop after an assignment is made?**

By phone and by assignment letter. A deadline is given. We ask authors to let us know if they have trouble. We can put our heads together to solve problems. The best thing a writer can do is listen well and pay attention to the assignment. The worst is when a writer takes off on his own and has a great time, but doesn't write the article that we asked for.

□ **What can an editor do to keep the writer on track?**

If we're not sure about the writer, we might ask for an outline. Also, we can usually tell if the story is on track just by talking to the writer on the phone.

□ **Should writers panic if they can't make the deadline?**

Yes, they should panic a little. We try to assign articles way ahead of schedule. If an author is in trouble, I want to know immediately. If I was going to use that story for a given issue, I can then plan accordingly. I will be slightly annoyed, but we can adapt. With more warning, we can adapt better.

□ **Once an article is published, how does the writer know that the piece was successful? Will you communicate with the writer?**

The only way we'll communicate with the writer is if we get letters from readers about the story. We send those letters to the writer.

□ **Do you have pet peeves about things that writers do?**

Yes. Submissions from writers who have not done their research. I don't want a story about a 4- or 5-year-old-child. That's not what we do. I'm also not crazy about writers who are very pushy and won't take no for an answer. I don't want to be pushed. I also don't like writers who make false claims. Let's have truth in advertising in the query or cover letter. If a writer says, "This happened to me. This never happened to another mom," and I get into the manuscript to find that it's the most common story in the world, that writer lied.

□ **Do you have advice for beginning writers?**

For a first-time writer, I prefer to see the manuscript. A manuscript will tell me whether this person can write. It takes me a page and a half of reading the manuscript to tell whether I like it. If a manuscript is decent, but not as snappy or well written as we'd like, we can fine tune it. If the idea is really good, we may be willing to do that.

□ **Do you have advice to writers about how to deal with editors?**

As anxious as writers are to know what's happening with their story, they have to understand how busy editors are. Most writers have no idea what editors go through. Even the best-run magazines encounter snags and have panic times.

The slush piles up. A manuscript that was sent in over the transom is a very low priority.

Freelancers have to give it a few months. We do the best we can. It's not that we're trying to ignore writers. We've tried a million things. We've said, "All right, Friday afternoons we're going to attack the slush pile." Well, Friday afternoon comes and we're behind the eight ball on a story and, again, the slush pile doesn't get read.

11

Writing for the Seven Sisters

SUSAN UNGARO, EDITOR IN CHIEF
Family Circle
New York

SUSAN UNGARO holds undergraduate and master's degrees in communication arts. Her first job after graduate school was at *Family Circle*. She
worked her way up from assistant editor to editor in chief. Unlike most top
editors, she has been with the same publication for her entire professional
life (eighteen years). Ungaro was appointed editor in chief in March 1994.

Family Circle was started in 1932 as a free supermarket magazine. In the
beginning, the magazine published articles about food, but the covers were
celebrity-driven. "It was like a *People* magazine of its day with recipes
included," explains Ungaro. *Family Circle* gradually evolved to become
more of a women's "how to manage your life" publication without celebrity
gossip. "I think 'how to' are the magic words that many publications later
came to embrace," says Ungaro. "*Family Circle* is the ultimate how-to
women's magazine." She adds that *Family Circle* is a trusted source book for
the latest information on everything from food, home, finances, fashion,
and beauty, to the social issues that affect women today, including education, health, environment, and social trends. Published seventeen times a
year, *Family Circle* is sold in supermarkets and on newsstands as well as
through 2.5 million subscriptions, with a total circulation of 5 million.

☐ **What are the Seven Sisters? How did the name come about?**
The name "Seven Sisters" was given to us by the ad industry because our
magazines—*Family Circle*, *Woman's Day*, *Good Housekeeping*, *Ladies' Home Journal*, *McCall's*, *Redbook*, and *Better Homes & Gardens*—reach the largest number
of women in America today.

Family Circle is bought by 5 million readers every three weeks. *Woman's Day*'s average circulation is smaller than ours—4.6 million to 4.8 million. *Good Housekeeping* sells 5 million copies. *Ladies' Home Journal* is the same. *Redbook* sells 3 million, *Better Homes & Gardens* goes to 7 million, and *McCall's* reaches about 5 million people per issue. Over the years, other magazines have tried to become the eighth sister.

The problem is that plenty of other women's magazines have some of the same kinds of editorial focus as the Seven Sisters, but they have a much smaller circulation—one million and under—or they're targeted to a younger audience, such as *Glamour* or *Mademoiselle*. The median age of most of Seven Sisters' readers is in the forties. *Redbook* readers are a little younger, from thirty-eight to forty years old.

◻ You're talking about a huge readership among the Seven Sisters.
When you're selling 5 million copies of the magazine, "pass-along" readership is much larger. We all have about 17 million to 26 million readers per copy. That is the largest audience of women. It's a rare television show that reaches that many people.

◻ How does *Family Circle* differ from *Woman's Day?*
Ah. The big question. That's like asking how *Time* differs from *Newsweek*. *Family Circle* and *Woman's Day* have different voices. We emphasize family concerns with our "Family Answer Book" series and offer inspiring "Can-Do" profiles of "Women Who Make a Difference" in every issue. I believe we are a magazine that has made advocacy journalism a priority. We're the only one of our "sisters" to win the prestigious ASME and Sigma Delta Chi awards for public interest reporting.

◻ How are the Seven Sisters similar and how are they different?
Woman's Day and *Family Circle* have the largest newsstand circulation. We are distributed in the supermarket venue to a much greater extent than *McCall's*, *Redbook*, *Ladies' Home Journal*, *Good Housekeeping*, or *Better Homes & Gardens*. The majority (80%–90%) of their readership is subscription-based.

The demographics of the Seven Sisters are very close. The *Family Circle* reader is, demographically speaking, the same reader as the *Ladies' Home Journal* or the *Good Housekeeping* reader. But we all have unique columns and features.

◻ Does this mean that information about being published in *Family Circle* will be information applicable to being published in the six other Sisters?
Most of the information that I give you would work well for writers for the Seven Sisters and the other major women's magazines.

□ **How do you usually acquire articles?**

Two ways. The editors come up with ideas and give assignments to writers with whom we have established working relationships. Or, writers send us query letters on important subjects that they think would make good stories for *Family Circle*. Fifty percent of our articles are written by freelancers.

□ **Does someone at *Family Circle* read every query that comes in over the transom?**

Someone reads everything in the slush pile. Junior editors go through the mail and pull out queries that are right for us. The rest get a form letter response. Because we read all queries, this means that first-time writers have an excellent chance of getting published in *Family Circle*.

□ **How can new writers break in at the big magazines?**

Writers with a new angle, new pitch, or new hook have a very good chance of being assigned an article. A great way for a new writer to break in is to come up with a clever idea for tackling seasonal stories.

Certain "evergreen" articles are published in every magazine over and over again. For instance, we constantly tell readers different ways to make the most of their money or to take charge of their health. I do a story every spring and fall on spring cleaning your house, how to get organized, how to deal with the clutter in your life. Romance and marriage secrets—how to make your marriage closer, more intimate, more loving—are probably addressed in every issue of every women's magazine, not just the Seven Sisters. Writers could also play up little known surveys concerning new ways to make a marriage more loving.

I constantly tell writers, don't send your ideas to the executive editor or the editor in chief. The best way to break in as a new writer is to pick a name that's lower down on the masthead. Try to develop a relationship with a younger editor. A younger editor's job is to bring in new ideas and new talent to make a name for himself or herself. That junior editor will pitch ideas to the senior editor and ultimately to the editor in chief.

The writer who completes an assignment and does a good job will have a foot in the door for future assignments.

□ **What sparks your interest in a query that comes in over the transom?**

An interesting title sparks my interest. Rather than saying, "I'd like do a story on why women should get more medical exams," start off your query with a provocative statistic (I'm making this one up and it's not an accurate statement): "25% of Women Who Die of Breast Cancer Could Have Survived If They Had Only Had a Mammogram When They Were 35 Years Old." If I read a query letter with that kind of a statement based on a new study that the writer read about in JAMA or another medical journal, I'd read further.

A provocative query letter is essential. You're selling your idea to the editor. Think about what advertisers do on television to get you to buy products. Think about what happens at the grocery store when you're walking down the aisle— why you pick up one cereal box or one box of cookies instead of another. Chances are it might have something to do with the packaging and the presentation. I'm not talking about writing a query letter on fancy stationery. It's much more about a quick, to-the-point, interesting title, unique point of view, and if there's something exclusive, that's even better.

□ What happens after you decide to publish an article?

If the writer wrote a query, the editor will discuss the idea and what we're expecting that article to achieve. Next, there will be a discussion over the phone, where all negotiations happen. We call you to say, "We really like your idea about 'Five Medical Tests That Can Save a Woman's Life.' But along with what you included in your proposal, we'd like you to add a sidebar reporting ten other tests that every woman should consider getting."

Information from that conversation should be put in writing. At *Family Circle*, the writer gets an assignment letter from the editor. This assignment letter will include information on the angle, the length, and an outline for the article that was discussed during the phone conversation. The assignment letter is mailed to the writer with the contract (which states the deadline—usually one or two months) and with what we call our fact-checking guidelines. We also give writers computer compatibility guidelines.

□ How much money do the Seven Sisters magazines pay freelance writers?

On average, fifty cents to a dollar per word, depending on a writer's experience. We pay upon acceptance of the article. Acceptance means after revisions.

□ What about expenses?

Expenses should be agreed on up front when the editor calls to assign a story. Editors know whether there will be expenses involved. If you live in California and the subjects of your story live in Wyoming, there will be some travel expenses involved.

□ Do you pay kill fees?

Of course, but we don't want to do that. *Family Circle* has very few kill fees because of our assignment letters. All expectations are laid out up front. Our desire is to make the story work. A lot of kill fees are paid because there wasn't a clear statement of what was expected from the story and the writer wrote with little or no direction. There are times, of course, when a writer can't deliver. That's unfortunate. Our kill fee is the industry average of 20 percent.

□ What rights do you offer?

It depends. Every publication wants all rights. It's negotiation from there. The first time you write for *Family Circle* you're probably going to give us all print rights. If you're an experienced writer with an agent, you may say you only want to give us first North American serial rights and always consider that. But if it's our idea that was generated in-house and we give the exclusive to the story to a writer with whom we have a relationship, chances are that we're going to negotiate for more rights than just first North American. We also have recently revised our writers contracts to include possible ways to reprint articles in books, on-line for additional compensation.

□ What are your pet peeves about writers?

People who write lazy query letters or writers who submit the same idea simultaneously to several publications. If you have an incredible exclusive and you are sending multiple submissions, at least say it in the letter.

Writers who pitch a story that is obviously not right for *Family Circle*. If it seems they haven't read *Family Circle*, they're less likely to hit a home run on the query.

□ Do you have final advice for writers who want to be published in *Family Circle* or the other Seven Sisters magazines?

Make the editor feel that you understand the magazine.

Think of yourself as a salesperson for yourself. The editor is the salesperson for her job. My senior editors are constantly pitching me ideas just like you're pitching ideas to them. They want to come up with the best story ideas and the most clever angles on the most extraordinary narratives. Make your idea stand out, even if it's an evergreen subject.

Writers should put themselves in the editor's place. We want our readers to read a story. How do we get them to read a story? We give the story the most provocative title we can imagine. We edit the feature so that it has the most interesting lead we can give the story. The art director and the designers design pages that pop and invite the reader to stay interested. Writers should make their query letter pop and sound interesting as well.

Finally, I'm always looking for what I call the "crackerjack" factor: a surprise in every issue. Make yours a crackerjack query.

12

Magazines: The Past, the Present, and the Future

How Publishing Has Changed, the Future, Electronic Publishing, How Freelance Writers Can Survive, and More

CLAY FELKER, FORMER EDITOR

Life and *Esquire*

Founder and Editor of *New York*

New York

CLAY FELKER graduated from college with a degree in political science. He began his publishing career as a sports writer at *The Sporting News* at the now-defunct *New York Daily Star* and *Life* magazine. After a stint at *Life*'s Washington, D.C. bureau, Felker returned to New York as *Esquire*'s articles editor. He then went to the *Herald Tribune* as editor of its Sunday magazine, *New York Magazine*. When the *Tribune* merged with the *World Telegram* and the *Journal American* in 1968, Felker founded *New York* magazine as an independent publication. After Rupert Murdoch bought *New York*, Felker, with a partner, purchased *Esquire* and became its editor. Since that time, Felker has worked for Twentieth Century Fox, developing stories for movies, and was editor of the afternoon edition of the *New York Daily News*. In addition, he was been editor of *AdWeek*, *Manhattan, Inc.*, and M magazine. Felker presently teaches journalism at the graduate school of the University of California–Berkeley and is director of The Felker Magazine Center.

□ **How has magazine publishing changed, and what do you see for the future?**

Magazine publishing has changed primarily in the creation of targeted vehicles—specialty magazines. The day of the general-interest magazine is rapidly drawing to a close. None of them makes money. The few that are left are losing money because of the competition—television and broadcast. Also, we're in an automobile culture. People who commute to work in their cars can't read magazines. The time that people have to read magazines is shrinking. Consumers will buy a specialized magazine when their interest lies in that area. Magazines will not be read unless they directly and very strongly reflect a reader's vital interest.

□ **Are specialty magazines helping the magazine publishing industry to survive?**

That's exactly what's happening. There's actually an explosion in the magazine business. There are more magazines now than ever before in American history—over thirty thousand magazines. The specialty magazines that are doing well are in areas like information technology, computers, hobbies, and business.

□ **Are there differences between men and women in terms of magazine preference?**

Men are more interested in specialized subjects like sports and finance. Women are interested in these areas, too, but they also look to women's magazines for service.

□ **Will on-line services replace magazines in the future?**

Nothing is going to replace the printed page. Most magazines are looking to go on-line, but that will create a different product. Although it would stem from the same knowledge base, on-line magazine service would be an entirely different [concept].

□ **What do you advise freelance writers, especially in view of changes that are occurring in the magazine industry?**

Construct a good query. An editor is likely to respond to a well-constructed, well-thought through query.

Focus your story.

Become expert in an area. Writers must be able to examine a field intelligently and provide more insight and knowledge than a general assignment reporter. A good writer will know a subject so well that he or she can tell practitioners in a field something that they don't already know.

□ **What area is good for freelance writers?**

One of the strongest areas is business. About half of all American magazines are about business. There are not enough business reporters.

□ **What special knowledge will help magazine freelancers be published?**

Magazines vary not only by specialty but by attitude. Values and attitudes are one of the central services that a magazine brings to its readers. *U.S. News & World Report* appeals to the values and attitudes of its audience differently than *Time* and *Newsweek*. Although *Spin* magazine and *Rolling Stone* both cover the pop music field, they have different attitudes. A magazine's subject matter is interpreted through the values and attitudes of its audience.

13

Magazines and the Information Superhighway

RICHARD DUNCAN, EXECUTIVE EDITOR

Excalibur, the Time, Inc.
Online Information Service
New York

RICHARD DUNCAN was an English major in college. After graduating from the Columbia School of Journalism in 1961, Duncan worked for the Associated Press. He then went to South America on a journalism fellowship. After he returned, he spent a short time at *Newsweek* before settling in at *Time*, where he climbed the editorial ladder from trainee/correspondent to executive editor. Duncan is in charge of *Time*'s online and new media activities.

Time magazine was founded in 1923 by Henry Luce. *Time*'s present weekly circulation is 4.2 million.

☐ **Does *Time* accept freelance contributions?**
We do, but we usually assign stories to writers we know. Over the transom doesn't happen. Many regular contributors listed on our masthead are former staffers and we have a stable of essayists who write for the back of the magazine, but we are gradually dealing more with outside writers that we contact personally.

☐ **Tell me about magazine publishing as it relates to the new media, online, CD-ROM, and all of those new technologies. How are *Time* and other magazines breaking in and evolving?**
At the initial stage, in 1993, the contents of magazines were put on CD-ROM or on-line. It was very simple and very inexpensive, but not very satisfactory. It was

primitive because we were experimenting. *Time* has now gone a step further. We created a daily on-line *Time* news summary, which offers information plus a spin to the daily news. It has been quite successful.

Magazines can no longer just throw their content on-line and say take it or leave it. The audience won't take it. Magazines have begun to tailor information for the new medium. That works much better. It has also created some jobs for writers. Several people write for our on-line magazine.

☐ **What is the most important aspect of the new media that can't be accomplished on the printed page?**

Very fast delivery. It's demographics. We can now reach people who were tuned out on the printed page.

☐ **Is the fast-paced growth of computer networks the reason magazines have turned to the information superhighway?**

Yes. America Online had about 300,000 subscribers in 1993. It now has over 2.5 million. There's a tremendous surge of growth and dynamism in these networks. They are growing across the country as fast as computers with modems. And every year the number of computers with modems in the United States doubles. You can't plug in any figures like that in printed magazine readership. Magazine circulation is generally static.

☐ **Will on-line magazines be a good market for freelance writers?**

I doubt it. We're talking about tailoring information, which requires people working together. That must be done in-house by a magazine's staff. I wouldn't consider going to a freelance writer for that work.

☐ **Can freelancers expect to get paid for the electronic publishing of an article that was published in a magazine?**

The position taken by most publishers is that they should not. Putting content on-line is, in legal terms, an extension of the initial publishing act or publishing by other means. But it is not a separate publication, so no rights or extra money is due the writer. That case is presently being tested in the New York federal courts. It's a very important principle that should be decided in several years. It's going to take a long time. Let me add, however, that presently very little freelance material is going on-line. It's not a big deal now, but it will probably be a big deal in the future.

☐ **What kind of writing is suitable for on-line publishing? What kind of writing is not?**

Short and punchy pieces with a higher tone of voice are good for on-line use. A higher tone of voice means an aggressive vocabulary and increased use of emotional words. On-line systems respond to the shorter attention span of the

American user. Of course, there are literate and intelligent people on-line. Laid-back or amusing articles found in print publications are not appropriate for on-line publishing. By and large, users won't read long articles, screen after screen, scrolling through a little window on a computer.

□ **Do you have advice for writers in dealing with the new media?**
If I were a freelance writer, I'd think about the future and I'd pick up skills from screen writing. I'd learn to write short, punchy bursts of descriptive material as well as text that accompanies images because moving images are next. Moving images—video and digitized video—are coming soon.

Part Two

The Magazines

14

Writing for *The Washingtonian* and Other City Magazines

JACK LIMPERT, EDITOR

The Washingtonian
Washington, D.C.

JACK LIMPERT let law school help him decide on a career in journalism. He quit after a year at Stanford to join the ranks of reporters at United Press International News Service. After four years with UPI, he worked for a variety of newspapers. In 1968 Limpert received a Congressional Fellowship and assisted Hubert Humphrey during his presidential campaign. In January 1969 he became editor of *The Washingtonian* magazine.

The Washingtonian, founded in October 1965, has a paid monthly circulation of over 165,000.

□ **What are city magazines?**
City magazines can be divided into big, medium, and small, depending on the size of the city. We describe *The Washingtonian* as "the magazine Washington lives by." City magazines help readers understand their city. They usually present a different point of view than local newspapers.

□ **How do city magazines differ from one another?**
A metropolitan area of 3 million or more can support a city magazine of over 100,000 circulation, a critical mass in terms of staff size and magazine quality. *The Washingtonian* serves the Washington, D.C. area with its population of 3.5 million. Cities that are closer to 2 million in metro area population tend to have magazines that are 50,000 to 60,000 circulation. They have much smaller staffs

and a harder time making a profit. Then there's a group of even smaller city magazines, which usually have only one or two key people who do almost everything.

□ How do big city magazines like *The New Yorker* and *New York* differ from magazines like *The Washingtonian*?

The New Yorker and *New York* have become much more national. *The Washingtonian* is a metropolitan area magazine. Our interest is local, not national. We reach out regionally, but not far. Our advertising base is mostly local.

□ Is *The Washingtonian* more staff-written or freelance-written?

We are heavy on staff and light on freelance. In time, we'd like a smaller staff and a bigger group of freelancers. Freelance writers bring in vitality and freshness. Generally city magazine editors usually buy stories from freelancers who live in the area because they want writers to bring in-depth knowledge of their city. A successful city magazine connects with its own city and directly affects the lives of its readers. *The Washingtonian* almost never accepts contributions from anyone outside our area because we can find the writers we need right here. We also wouldn't publish a story about environmental problems in the Rocky Mountains, for example. Our environmental story will be on the Potomac River or on our air quality.

□ What's more important, a writer's literary style or journalistic skills?

It depends on the story. In an environmental story, reporting and thinking would be more important than the writing. The writing must be clear, but you don't have to be Tom Wolfe to do an air quality piece.

□ Do city magazines publish travel pieces?

Some do. We publish a cover story each year called "Great Weekends" or "52 Getaways" or something like that. We occasionally buy pieces from travel writers, but they're usually local.

□ What do you look for in an article?

Good reporting, good writing, good thinking, and maybe some passion. We look for something that lifts an article out of the ordinary.

□ What do you want in the query letter?

It should be addressed to somebody. An editor is turned off by a writer who has not looked at the magazine. A writer should interest the editor in an idea and then show a track record with clips of previously published work.

□ Do you offer a contract for each article you assign?

No. We exchange letters. We discuss the story, length, time, and money. We buy one-time rights.

□ **How much do you pay for articles?**
We pay about fifty cents per word, occasionally more if there's lots of research involved.

□ **What are your pet peeves?**
One is the writer who asks me to read a piece immediately. I usually read manuscripts at night or when I'm off deadline or I may ask another editor to look at it. Writers should give editors a decent amount of time to respond and then be pleasantly persistent.

□ **What do you want from writers other than writing ability?**
The writer must be a fair-minded person with no conflict that could embarrass the magazine. I don't want to get burned by a writer who has a financial or public relations interest in a story. I want writers to deliver on their promises and add info as indicated.

I also want writers who show enthusiasm. We look for good reporting and clear thinking, and we appreciate and reward enthusiasm.

15

Writing for *Yankee* and Other Regional Magazines

JIM COLLINS, SENIOR ASSOCIATE EDITOR
Yankee
Dublin, New Hampshire

JIM COLLINS graduated from Dartmouth College in 1984 with a degree in English. After graduation, he served as an editorial intern at *Yankee* magazine and was assigned to a start-up publication called *Yankee Homes*. After his year-long internship, he was appointed editor, a position he held until the magazine folded four years later. Collins then freelanced as a writer and editor of several major magazines until August 1993, when he returned to *Yankee* as senior associate editor.

Founded in 1935, *Yankee* is a mass-circulation, general-interest, regional magazine with a monthly circulation of 700,000.

☐ **Is *Yankee* a typical regional magazine?**
Yankee is a regional publication, but it doesn't fit perfectly in that category because our circulation spreads across the country. *Yankee* continues to be a general-interest magazine while other regional magazines have gone toward lifestyle. We publish poetry, fiction, full-length profiles, history, and off-beat and eclectic stories that have nothing to do with home, food, and travel, the mainstays of most other regional magazines. We also publish profiles of eccentric New England people—inventors or educators who are bucking a trend, for example. We publish a regional "sense of place" story each month. It might be a local battle over keeping open a one-room school in a small New England town.

Although *Yankee's* subject matter is strictly defined as New England (the six New England states) and its culture and history, there's something mythic about New England. This part of the country has a lot of character associated with it— ingenuity, independence, taciturnity, history. New England is where the country was born and where the seasons are so well defined. *Yankee* is a connection with New England for people who live outside the region. Once people have been to New England, they're often nostalgic for it, sometimes even before they leave. We survive because of the loyalty of our readers. We have not had to change our editorial plan to become more commercial, more trendy, or more advertising-driven.

□ Do all your writers live in New England?
Our mainstay of writers live here. That doesn't necessarily mean they were born and brought up here. We recently published an article about Hannah Duston, a historical figure who was captured by Indians but escaped after she scalped her captors. The author was one of her descendants. In the same issue was an article about a high school basketball team in a small Maine fishing village. Basketball defined that community and became more important than just a sport. Once you've lived in New England for a number of years, you begin to understand subtle things that you'll be able to bring into the writing that someone who has just flown in from New York or the Midwest will miss. We almost never publish stories that don't take place in New England.

□ Can new writers break in at *Yankee*?
It's possible, but not probable. About 75 percent of our articles usually go to an established pool of people who have written for us before or whose work we've read in other good magazines. For instance, as I read *The New Yorker*, *Esquire*, or *Outside*, I look for New England connections and New England bylines. I'll go after those writers for *Yankee*. Editors are not scouring the streets for unpublished writers and untried talent. We receive about thirty-five queries and thirty-five manuscripts a week. That's just nonfiction. Fiction submissions are even higher. Of the two thousand annual nonfiction submissions, no more than ten or twelve pieces will get published by a new writer a year and those will probably be very short pieces.

□ Does someone read everything that comes in over the transom?
Yes. Our entry-level editors serve as first readers. A surprising number of queries are immediately rejected because they don't take place in New England or because an idea is a standard chestnut that we get every week, a subject that is too cliché. A certain number of queries overlap with stories that were published recently or are in the works.

Queries that have promise are summarized and dropped in a picnic basket. Editors read everything in the basket in preparation for our Thursday morning editorial meetings, when we make the decisions. If the idea is a surprise or especially interesting, it will jump out. We then look at what the writer sees as the story. If it's about a lobster man off the coast of Maine, what makes that story unusual? If the writer can come up with meaning behind the subject and can convince us that there's something epic, ironic, odd, historical, or unusual, we may take a chance.

We also look at the writer's relationship with an idea. For example, the writer may say, "I lived in this neighborhood in the north end of Boston for the past twenty-eight years. I've watched a particular woman every day doing such and such." If we like the idea, we'll have to go with that writer because he or she has had that personal experience. If we want the idea, we have to take the writer with it.

□ **What if you take a chance on a new writer and the piece needs a lot of work?**
If the writer has no control of the writing or is disorganized and unprofessional, we will usually kill the piece. If the article just needs reworking or rethinking, we'll ask the writer to revise it.

□ **Give me an example of a query that you loved.**
Here's one. I pulled this one out of my files.

"For several years I have been playing with an idea that may be of interest to *Yankee*. When I break away from my everyday work (I'm a nature writer and photographer), I track major league baseball, occasionally going to games when time and geography permit. I keep a ballpark bird list. Last April, for instance, at Jim Abbott's Anaheim debut in California, a game he lost 7–0, a flock of Vaux's swifts combed moths out of the twilight sky above the stadium. These small sooty-colored birds were a life bird for me, a bird I'd hoped to catch as it migrated through the Mojave, but was delighted to find wheeling above the Angels and Mariners game in Anaheim. This was the first life bird I have ever seen at a major league stadium." The writer goes on and pitches a story about doing a bird-watcher's guide to Fenway Park in Boston, saying, "I love baseball, and I love birds, and Fenway Park is one of the best ballparks in the country to watch birds."

That juxtaposition caught my attention and we ended up running the story as a cover story. That is an example of a query that combines unlikely things and uses the writer's skills and strengths as a bird watcher and baseball fan. The idea was unusual and unexpected. We had to go with this writer. Who else could write the piece for us?

□ If you kill a piece, will you give the writer a kill fee?

Yes, but we're getting away from kill fees. We don't feel it's fair to writers who do the pieces they're asked to do and then we kill them for some other reason.

□ If an article sent on spec from a first-time writer is successful, will you assign that person another piece and then offer a contract?

I would think so. The only caveat is the writer with a special situation, such as the one in North Boston. If the writing didn't impress us, it's unlikely that we'll use him or her again.

□ Do you offer a contract for each article you assign?

Yes, except for a section of the magazine that publishes short bits and pieces that are only about 100 or 150 words.

□ How much do you pay for articles?

On average, for a feature article (about 2,500 words) we will pay in the range of 75 cents per word—$1,500 to $2,000 for that piece. Less for shorter pieces.

□ What are your pet peeves about writers?

I'm really turned off when a beginning writer has the arrogance to assume that we're going to buy a story before we've made the decision and immediately starts talking about money, deadlines, or photographs.

Most of the editors at *Yankee* resent outsiders telling us something about New England that we know is untrue or is an outsider's stereotypical perspective.

Surprisingly few writers are willing to do a lot of leg work or investigative reporting. Writers seldom say, "Here's a story that's going to involve a lot of reporting, a lot of investigative work, and I have not only the skills to do that but I'll make the time to do it well." Most unsolicited material is personal essays—"how wonderful it is to live in the country, how I grew my garden last year, how I got through the blizzard of 1978."

□ What do you advise writers who want to be published in *Yankee* or comparable magazines?

Before you send a query or manuscript, think about what makes you the only writer for that idea. We're not going to send an unpublished writer to cover the Freedom Trail in Boston. We've thought about that idea a thousand times. A new writer must come to us with an idea that only he or she could do—a personal perspective or situation.

Send clips. Clips always help, especially if they are from magazines that value good writing.

Phone calls following up a query are okay as long as the writer is humble. A gentle reminder without making us feel guilty for not having gotten back sooner is a good approach.

Our editor in chief believes that every person has one story to tell. A beginning writer should try to think of the one story that defines himself or herself. That story might have a chance here. We'll give the story more weight than we'll give the writer's name.

□ **What qualities do you look for in writers?**
A sense of humor, irony, the ability to tell a story, and control.

16

Writing for *American Way* and Other Airline Magazines

JEFF POSEY, FORMER SENIOR EDITOR AND FICTION EDITOR

American Way
Dallas

JEFF POSEY describes his career path as contorted. He graduated from college with a degree in geology, worked for five years with a Dallas oil company, and then entered the University of North Texas with hopes of earning a master's degree in journalism. After his first year of graduate school, Posey worked as an intern at *D* magazine, accepted a job there as a full-time editor and fact-checker, was quickly promoted to city editor, and gave up the master's program. In 1990, Posey joined *American Way* as associate editor. At the time of this interview Jeff Posey was senior editor and fiction editor of *American Way*.

Founded in 1966, *American Way* was the first in-flight magazine. Now published twice a month, each issue of *American Way* is read by 1.7 million American airlines passengers.

☐ **How have airline magazines changed and evolved with changes in travel?**
Fifteen to twenty years ago one airline magazine could not be distinguished from another. They were all essentially in-house organs published to convince customers to use their product. All good in-flight magazines have evolved beyond that to entertaining customers, not trying to convince them to take another trip.

□ What types of nonfiction articles does *American Way* publish?

We publish people and places stories. The people element is usually interviews and quotes that give a perspective on places. We don't do straight profiles. The place element is not necessarily a place profile or even a destination story. We want the viewpoint of people—natives, locals, experts, or the writer—within the realm of place. We would never run a story about Mexico City, for example, because a story that large would be nebulous and boring. We don't run stories about politics or religion.

□ Is *American Way* a good market for fiction writers?

Yes. All fiction is done on spec. We publish one piece of fiction in each issue with a limit of 2,500 words. Our fiction is akin to classical storytelling. The characters are well developed and motivated. They want something. They have obstacles and deal with those obstacles. They either get what they want or they don't.

□ What percent of *American Way* is freelance-written?

We're 98 percent to 99 percent freelance-written.

□ Tell me about the queries you receive.

We receive in the neighborhood of two hundred queries a week and they're usually of two types. There are queries from writers who don't know anyone on staff and clearly have made no effort to find a specific editor to send a query to. Those have the lowest chance of getting anywhere. The others are from writers who have obviously looked at a sample issue and submitted their query to a correctly spelled, named editor on staff. All queries are looked at by a very talented assistant editor who pulls out those that are good. The extreme bulk of the queries go back to the senders.

I turn down, without reading any further, queries from writers who just want to take a trip on our airline. "I want to fly to France to find out if there are any spas there," that writer might say. Well, of course there are spas in France. That query will be automatically rejected. If we manage to remember the writer's name, the next time we see his or her query we won't consider it. Writers can seriously hurt themselves by coming at us with a very shallow pitch.

□ What sparks your interest in certain queries?

I like queries from writers who are excited about the ideas they're pitching. I can get that feeling in their letter. Writers can convince me by demonstrating their longstanding interest or expertise in a subject. That really catches my eye. Someone who is passionate about something will probably write a better story.

The freelancer should let his or her natural writing ability flow into the query letter. Clarity is the root cause of all style. If the writing is clear, the writing style will reflect through.

□ What do you look for in a writer's clips?

I want to see a writer's best two to five single stories. I don't want every single story that he or she has published. I've received queries from writers who had good skills, but many of the fifty clips they sent were not very good. That made me doubt their judgment and their professionalism. I've occasionally made the decision not to use a writer who has sent too many clips.

□ How do you usually choose writers?

To coin a word, we're a "writer-centric" magazine. We spend more time, energy, and mental effort acquiring writers than stories. We choose freelancers on their ability to tell complicated stories in simple, understandable ways. Although we don't pay top rates, we want writers who work in the top-rate markets.

□ If you don't pay top rates, why will top writers work for *American Way?*

Because we simplify the editorial process. Our writers set the tone of the magazine. We don't have a specific writing style that we expect them to mimic. We let their personalities reflect through their writing. We are very receptive to their story ideas. Other magazines go through several tiers of editing. We don't. That's how we grab hold of and keep writers.

□ How do you test new writers so they can be published and eventually become regular contributors?

New writers go through a simple procedure. They write the first piece, which we edit and offer very careful feedback on. We try to be completely honest and straightforward. If they respond as professionals to our criticism, we will assign them a story. At this second stage, writers must show that they understand what we want, they must be pleasant to work with, and they must meet their deadlines. Once we've assigned an article to a first-time writer, he's got a foot in the door but not his whole leg. My rule of thumb is that a writer should successfully complete three good articles to become a regular contributor.

□ Why are some writers rejected from your regular pool?

They may have submitted articles with major factual problems. Or their stories may have come in ragged the first time and I had to lean hard on them for a good second or third draft. That's acceptable the first time. The second time, I begin to doubt them. If I have to do it a third time, I begin to wonder if this person is worth dealing with. I have taken writers through even the forth and fifth story stage before I decided that they couldn't crank out a good, high-quality first draft. Leaning on writers takes a lot of energy and effort. I'm not willing to do that on a continuing basis.

□ **Do you look with favor on writers who are technical experts or hold specialized degrees?**

No. That's almost a red flag. I tend to be prejudiced against people with technical experience. They often have difficulty writing a general-interest story.

□ **How much do you pay writers?**

We pay a little less than a dollar per word plus expenses for nonfiction and $900 flat rate for fiction, no expenses.

□ **Tell me about your contracts.**

We offer first worldwide English serial rights for every article. We put the word "worldwide" in there because our planes fly all over the world.

□ **What about kill fees?**

If a story is not used, our kill fee is one-quarter of the full fee. If a first story is killed, the writer will have a hard time getting published in our magazine again, except where there were extenuating circumstances beyond the control of the stylistic and reportorial ability of the writer.

□ **Do you have pet peeves about writers?**

One pet peeve is people who say, "I've seen a similar story in your magazine." The question they're really asking is, "Why don't you do it again?" In fact, we tend to think the other way. We've done a particular topic recently and we're not going to do it again. I know what these writers are trying to do. They're implying that they are familiar with our magazine. But they're not familiar with the way magazines work.

My biggest pet peeves are with established writers who think they're the next Hemingway and that any small criticism I give them is not justified. We won't use arrogant writers. I go way out of my way to give a very clear, straightforward, honest appraisal of a piece when it comes in. I try to offer opinions from the perspective of the reader. I rarely just say, "fix it." I might tell them, "I got confused here. I stumbled there. I don't know what you're talking about." Most writers handle criticism well, but some writers go ballistic. That really irritates me and I won't deal with those writers under any circumstance. I don't care how good they are.

I have a real problem when writers don't shoot straight with me, when they promise one thing and deliver another. That's unprofessional. If that writer had let me know about the problem, we could have figured something out.

□ **What do you advise writers who want to be published in *American Way* or airline magazines in general?**

Writers who have never been published before should be published in other magazines. You're not going to be published in *American Way* if you have no professional experience as a writer. Who would take a chance on somebody like that?

The main thing I look for in a freelancer is writing ability. If I don't see good writing, good storytelling narrative, and good reporting, I won't to do business with them. I don't care how good their ideas are.

It's often said that editors are gatekeepers. In effect, we are. I like to open the gate rather than close it. When I open the gate, I'm opening it to creative talent. I want those writers to use their whole ability to craft something into my magazine.

Writing for *Travel & Leisure* and Other Travel Magazines

KIM BROWN, SENIOR EDITOR
Travel & Leisure
New York

KIM BROWN was an English major in college. She got hooked on magazine publishing at a summer internship at *Mademoiselle*. After graduation, her first job was assistant to the editor at the now defunct *Savvy* magazine. "I was one of the worst secretaries on earth, but my boss let me do a lot, editorially," says Brown. "I saw how she put together a magazine—how she made assignments, handled revisions and contracts, and used her wonderful sense of humor with writers." In 1986 Brown joined *Travel & Leisure* as assistant editor. She was promoted to senior editor in March 1992.

Founded in 1971, Travel & Leisure is the largest consumer travel magazine in the United States. Its monthly circulation is just under one million.

☐ **How do you categorize *Travel & Leisure,* and how does it differ from competing travel publications?**
Travel & Leisure, *Condé Nast Traveler*, and *National Geographic Traveler* are all extremely upscale magazines. That means we cover the world of travel—resorts, hotels, restaurants, and luxury vacations—with style. But we all have very different personalities.

Condé Nast Traveler, our most direct competitor, does more reportorial work and investigative reporting—which airlines are the safest, what really happens to your luggage, how safe your hotel room is, what's the safest place to sit in a plane. *Condé Nast Traveler* is great at investigative how's and why's and the strategies of travel.

Travel & Leisure is more inspirational. It's why you should travel, not why you shouldn't. Our point of view is that you certainly might want to know that kind of information, but I have very little patience reading about why I shouldn't get on a plane. I want to know why I should get on and what I will do when I get off at the other end. *Travel & Leisure* has become more sophisticated over the years. Our readers have evolved and they are amazingly sophisticated about travel. As the readers change, the magazine changes. Our average reader is between the ages of forty and sixty.

National Geographic Traveler is somewhere between *Travel & Leisure* and *Condé Nast Traveler*. *National Geographic Traveler* is a much quieter magazine. I see their readers as older, less upscale—perhaps retired.

A fourth travel publication is *Travel Holiday*. It's comparable to *National Geographic Traveler*—a little more downscale, conservative, and older.

☐ Who writes for *Travel & Leisure*?

Ninety percent of our articles are written by freelancers. All major features are written by freelancers who have developed relationships with us. Most of our writers are well known.

☐ Do you receive many unsolicited, over-the-transom queries?

Yes. We probably receive more than fifty queries a week. We look at every one and usually respond in three to four weeks. Less than one percent are published.

☐ What's the best way for a new writer to break in at *Travel & Leisure*?

The best place to break in is one of *Travel & Leisure*'s two regional sections. We publish a western and an eastern edition of the magazine. We need four to six short (750 to 2,200 words), very focused travel features each month, written specifically for each of those editions. It's easier for writers who are breaking in at the magazine to query us with stories about places that are within a day's travel distance of where they live. For example, someone who lives in Vermont could submit new ideas about why someone would travel to Vermont—a new inn that hasn't been covered by the mainstream magazines or a new hiking area. In the California edition we might publish an article about a new cross-country ski destination outside San Francisco or an up-and-coming neighborhood in San Francisco.

☐ Should a writer query you before embarking on a big trip?

It's better to submit the query after the trip. The writer is in a better position to make his or her case—to say, "I've been there, it was incredible, the kind of people I bumped into were your readers." The query should be no more than one page. The writer might pitch three very specific ideas. The more specific, the better.

The query should be full of personality. Come up with something that's fresh, but not ridiculous. We're always looking for a fresh voice. Always include clips. Send at least a half-dozen clips. Magazine or newspaper clippings are acceptable, but we're drawn to magazine clips because they're similar to our style. They show us the writer's style and give the assigning editor more fuel.

□ Tell me about a query that won you over.

We published a piece in a regional slot called "Neighborhoods" about oddball museums in L.A. The author was a comedy writer in Los Angeles, and his letter had this great sense of humor. It was presented in an unusual way and was hilarious from the beginning. I could tell what the tone of the story would be from the query. The story was very funny.

□ Do you ever ask for stories on spec?

No. We never work on spec here. That's why it's so difficult for first-time writers to get assignments. Articles are always contracted. Once that assignment is made, it's a big deal.

□ Do you pay kill fees if an article doesn't work out?

We do pay kill fees. They're 25 percent. Kills are quite rare. We spend a lot of time making just the right assignment. Revision is standard procedure here.

□ How much do you pay freelance writers?

About one dollar per word.

□ What is a major mistake that new writers make?

A major mistake is not understanding how formatted most magazines can be these days. The departments and columns in *Travel & Leisure* are almost completely formatted. No column exists without a reason. We only take freelance material that fits those specific columns.

□ Do you have advice for writers who want to be published in *Travel & Leisure* and comparable magazines?

Learn about the magazine. That's crucial. Read several issues.

Send the query to the right editor. A blind query will most likely land on the wrong desk. It could be a month before it gets to the right desk. Call and charm an editorial assistant into telling you who edits which sections of the magazine and who assigns certain stories. That's 50 percent of the game at any magazine.

The query and the clips need to shine. The writer should keep in mind that an editor might have to pitch that article and make a case to several other editors as to why this story should be assigned. If the writer doesn't have a good idea to begin with, the editor is going to have a tough time. The writer needs to think through all pertinent questions. The writer must think like an editor—"not only why I want to write this, but why the magazine should publish it."

Writers must be extremely tenacious, patient, and persistent. It's a rare query that has the spark that will lead an editor to take the chance. But that's the fun of the editor's job—discovering new talent.

18

Writing for *Field & Stream* and Other Outdoor Magazines

MAGGIE NICHOLS, CONTRIBUTING EDITOR AND FORMER MANAGING EDITOR

Field & Stream
New York

MAGGIE NICHOLS holds undergraduate and master's degrees in English. After graduate school, she worked at a trade magazine called *Quick Frozen Foods* in New York. In 1961 she went to *Field & Stream*, where she climbed the ranks from assistant editor to managing editor, her position at the time of this interview. She has stepped down but works part-time as a Contributing Editor at *Field & Stream*.

Field & Stream was founded in 1895. "The magazine is the soul of the American outdoors," says Nichols. "That's our slogan." According to Nichols, *Field & Stream* fosters conservation, sportsmanship, love for the outdoors, and good hunting and fishing practices. The monthly circulation is 2 million.

□ **How do you categorize *Field & Stream?***
Field & Stream is a hunting and fishing magazine. It's heavy on the why-to's and the how-to's. We also publish a lot of conservation material and essays.

□ **What is your competition and how does *Field & Stream* stand out?**
Our major competition is *Outdoor Life* and *Sports Afield*. The differences are very subtle, but *Field & Stream* runs more of what I call "why-to"—articles that reveal the feeling of things. *Outdoor Life*, on the other hand, is more gear and straightforward how-to.

□ **Why have outdoor magazines like *Field & Stream, Outdoor Life,* and *Sports Afield* survived for one hundred years?**

Because they cater to a special interest. Special-interest magazines have the best chance of long-term survival. People need specialized information to help them enjoy their special interests and to keep up with new developments. They can't get that information on television or from general-interest magazines. Our readers are people who are actively interested in doing things outdoors; 80 percent of our readers are men.

□ **Are magazines like *Field & Stream* a good market for freelance writers?**

Yes, they are. The outdoor magazine field is very fertile. We buy good material and we buy a lot of it. We receive a lot of material from freelance writers who send queries. We receive fifty to seventy queries per week. A group of contributing editors regularly submits ideas to us, and we sometimes ask writers to submit pieces.

□ **How can writers break in at *Field & Stream?***

A first-time writer can break in by succinctly stating an idea that we have not just run. If it seems like a subject our readers will be interested in, it will have a good chance of being published. A good place for new writers to break in is "*Field & Stream* Junior"—four pages of interest to young people. We also want stories on trout fishing, bass fishing, deer and elk hunting, nature—virtually anything about hunting and fishing and the outdoors. The "By-the-Way" section runs short, how-to material. This area of the magazine eats up a lot of material. We take personal essays for the last page—the "Finally . . . " section. These are hard to write, since they must make a point—an epiphany of some sort—and not be simply anecdotal. And a section called "Guest Shot" could be a memory or nostalgia—something that grasps the essence of an outdoor experience such as trout fishing that is longer than the essay.

□ **Will you look at manuscripts as well as queries?**

Yes. It's sometimes best to send the article. For example, there's no way that you can query humor or essays. It's the writing that sells those pieces.

□ **What is your definition of a good query letter?**

A good query is no more than one or two pages and clearly defines what the writer plans to do. A query that says, "I want to do an article on deer hunting in Wisconsin" will not work. It must have a particular slant.

□ **How should a writer focus an article for *Field & Stream?***

The writer could talk about trout-fishing techniques practiced in a particular area, for example, and various ways to present a fly, tricks with spinning lures, and so on. He could demonstrate variations on a dry fly-fishing technique. Who knows? There are endless things that an active and expert fly fisherman might have discovered.

□ How much do you pay freelancers?

$800 and up for 1,000- to 1,500-word articles. Less for short features, fillers, and so on.

□ Do you offer a contract for every article?

Upon acceptance. We don't assign by contract except when we have instituted the idea. We pay on spec because though we may like a query, often the submitted article doesn't live up to the query. We almost always buy if the article as written is what the writer described in the query and if the writing meets our standards.

□ Do you have pet peeves?

Writers who obviously never read the magazine and don't have a clue as to what we publish. At least open the magazine. Look at the contents page and you'll see that we don't run pieces on rock climbing or hang gliding. It's clear when people have no idea of what we run.

Something that people do that's really dumb is look at old issues of magazines to see which editor to send material to. They'll look at magazines from the 1970s. It's incredible. What do they think—there's no turnover? Spend a couple of dollars or go to the library.

A writer who says, "I see you have trouble getting good articles." This will kill a query letter right off the bat. It's amazing what people think is clever.

It's most annoying to get a good query, accept it, and either never receive the article or get a piece that is nothing like the writer's description in the query.

Writers who call editors. No editor has time to talk on the phone. It's not a good idea to fax material either. Faxes get lost. They come out of that machine wrinkled or curled up on the floor. We don't have a huge staff. It's easier to handle the mail that comes in a big batch and we can sort it out. It just works better. The U.S. mail is the best way.

□ What endears certain writers to you?

Writers who take the trouble not only to look at the magazine, but to study it. It's obvious and it's very endearing.

People who write cleanly, write well, write short, and have something to say. These writers are going to get bought in an instant.

Writers who understand that every word in their piece isn't precious. Editors sometimes have to cut articles.

□ **What do you advise writers who want to be published in *Field & Stream* and comparable publications?**

If you have a story and don't know where to send it, get a bunch of magazines and read them carefully. See where your story might fit. Also, check out the last pages. Many magazines publish essays on those last pages.

Even writers who don't hunt and fish or don't have any particular knowledge of the subject could pick up ideas by reading the magazines. They may have a story that they didn't realize would fit in or they may know someone who could help them.

Freelancing is a horribly difficult job. We editors appreciate it. We need freelancers. Almost every magazine does. We will go out of our way to work with a writer if there's even a germ of a good idea. It's so nice for us when a writer works hard and writes a good tight piece that says something.

The magazine field is wonderful now. There are loads of new magazines coming out. Writers must realize, however, that editors won't buy material that isn't directed specifically to them.

19

Writing for *Country Journal*

Writing about the Country Life—Gardening, Nature, Conservation, and the Environment

PETER FOSSEL, EDITOR/ASSOCIATE PUBLISHER

Country Journal
Stamford, Connecticut

PETER FOSSEL's college major was political science. After graduation, he worked in the editorial departments of various newspapers. Fossel temporarily gave up the newspaper business to become a freelance writer. "I liked reporting and editing," says Fossel, "but I decided to try freelance writing rather than wait until I was seventy." Nevertheless, Fossel was soon hired as senior editor of a start-up magazine called *New Home*. The publication only lasted a year and a half, but Fossel learned how to run a magazine. In 1988 he joined *Country Journal* as senior editor. He then became editor, and in 1990 was named editor/associate publisher.

Country Journal was founded in 1974 by Richard M. Ketchum, a former editor of American Heritage Books, and William Blair, a former publisher of *Harper's*. Although there are now about twenty-five to thirty magazine titles on the newsstands with the word "country" in them, *Country Journal* remains successful in its twenty-second year. Its everincreasing bimonthly circulation ranges from 250,000 to 300,000.

□ **Tell me about *Country Journal*'s readers.**
Geographically, they cover the Frost Belt from Maine to Minnesota and then South to the colder regions of the Appalachians. That's a factor of our gardening

coverage. We can't cover gardening in the Everglades or Tucson. For some reason, we have a lot of readers from California and the Pacific Northwest.

□ How do you define today's *Country Journal?*

Country Journal is a literate service magazine for people who live with their land, who want to leave it in better shape than they found it, and who enjoy working it. *Country Journal* exists outside the back door. We deal with houses in terms of energy efficiency and alternative fuels. We cover the land, the barn, the garden, and nature. But we don't deal with furniture and furnishings. Our direct competitors are *Mother Earth News* and *Harrowsmith Country Life*. In special areas of coverage, such as gardening and the environment, there are many other magazines that nibble away at the edges.

□ What article ideas are you looking for?

We're looking for ideas that nobody else is doing and that will connect directly with our readers' lives. When a query comes in from a writer who says, "Would you like to hear about my two-year experience in the backwoods of Maine?" my response is, "Probably not." That is what I call a "How I spent my vacation" story. Unless the writer learned something valuable to pass on to readers, it's of no use to me.

We want stories that have inspirational value—I'm not talking about religion—but an affirmation so that readers will think, "My gosh, this person did this. I could do it, too. This person made $10,000 selling fruits and vegetables off the back of his pickup truck. I could do that. That person built his own house or built his own barn or started his own garden and never did it before. I could do that, too. I could do anything." All of us can do a lot more than we think we can. Part of our job at *Country Journal* is to let people know that they can do it. They can run their own lives. They can control their lives to a certain extent. We want ideas and articles that will inspire and teach our readers to do something they might not have thought they could do.

□ Give me examples of *Country Journal* topics.

We've published articles that range from home schooling to building an ice skating rink in your backyard, from planning a garden in January to life as a vegetarian. Health—physical or emotional—is part of our realm. Why do people move from the city to Vermont? In some way they want to live a healthier life.

I try to include at least one ruminative piece in each issue. Writers can't query on essays. I always scan through the essays that come in over the transom to see if one rises to the surface. Once in a while it does. We publish about five essays a year out of a couple hundred that are submitted.

☐ **How many queries and manuscripts do you receive over the transom?**
We receive more than fifty queries or manuscripts a week.

☐ **Do you ever publish anything just as it comes in?**
Beyond essays, we rarely publish any manuscripts as they arrive in the mail. Whether it's a query or manuscript, if it's a tremendous idea, we'll go back to the writer and say it's got real potential, but we'd like that elusive human factor, or it needs more anecdotes, or expand a little on this and cut that part, or answer these questions. Every magazine has an editorial character or tone or personality. It's usually the editor's personality, for better or worse. But it has that personality. But within that range, a writer can do all sorts of wild things.

☐ **How do you get most of your article ideas?**
We sit around and brainstorm in the office, but our ideas usually come from writers. We recast queries or manuscripts along the lines that work for *Country Journal*, but at the same time we always try to watch for a surprise that shouldn't be recast. For instance, we ran a story on midwives and home births. People probably weren't expecting that in our magazine. I like to surprise readers once in a while.

☐ **Do you have a group of writers on whom you depend?**
Yes. But they're not all writers. Some have other occupations. I'll call anybody. I once called the governor of Connecticut to ask him to write a short piece about running for local office.

☐ **What sparks your interest in a writer?**
Someone who comes up with a lead that makes me continue reading will impress me. Ninety percent of the battle is the lead. A writer who can summarize and tell readers what they're about to get into in that first paragraph—that's a gift. I offer a lot of money to people who can do that. The rest of the story usually meets expectations.

A writer is nothing more than a conduit of information from one source to another. A writer must sort out irrelevant information and pass along only what the reader needs to know. The language must be clear and concise. There must be no doubt about what the writer means to say.

But a writer must be human. At *Country Journal*, the best writing is conversation in text form that provides a human connection from one person to another. It's poetry in prose clothing. It conveys to the reader that we're all in that same boat. We've all been there. It must seem as if the writer is communicating by letter to one person—not to 300,000 anonymous people. Whether it's because of a turn of a phrase or the use of analogies, the recipient must enjoy reading that letter.

Writers must provide a sense of authority. Everything has to be factually correct. There must be no question about the authority behind the piece.

□ What do you want in query letter?

Brevity. One page is excellent. I want to enjoy reading the letter. I want to feel that the person is writing to me and I'm not just the latest name plucked out of the computer.

I don't have a formula for a query letter. Writers don't have to tell me how long the piece will be or why they think I should like the idea. Writers should not raise more questions than they answer in the query letter. If they do it in the letter, they'll do it in a text. And that's an unforgivable sin.

I want writers to present the idea and tell me enough about it so that I don't have to ask them to flesh it out. The query must provide sufficient information. I want to know, based on their letter alone, whether we should proceed with the piece.

I want clips from writers I haven't worked with. But the letter itself means a lot more than clips. I don't know from a clip if the writer or the editor really wrote the story.

The caliber of the query is what counts. The letter should be straightforward, forthright, and cover all bases. The writer should then get out of it—don't tune the fiddle for a paragraph and stay around to get applause at the end.

□ Is it okay for writers to call you if they haven't heard about their query?

Yes. If they haven't heard in a few weeks they ought to call and raise holy hell. I'll probably say we're loaded right now, bear with me, we haven't forgotten you.

□ How much do you pay freelance writers?

In the neighborhood of fifty cents per word. We'll negotiate. We'll make an offer and ask if it's fair. I want to be fair to writers. Writers are treated pretty badly by many magazines. We won't offer as much to a first-time writer as we would to somebody we've worked with before. If that writer does a bang-up job, we'll offer more next time. I want to keep writers happy and productive and writing for us.

□ Do you offer a contract for each piece?

Yes. I don't often ask for articles on spec, but I may ask it of first-time writers. I'll tell them, "You could be buying into a lot of work here. Our standards are high. But if you do want to write it, you'll have to do it on speculation. We might not buy the piece and I don't want you to feel resentful." I almost try to talk them out of it. If they say, "Okay, it's worth it," we'll give them a shot at it.

☐ **Do you offer kill fees?**

Yes. But very rarely. I hate to do that.

☐ **Tell me about your pet peeves.**

Number one pet peeve is when writers take ten words to say something they could say in one. Also, a piece that isn't organized or doesn't have a logical flow, carelessness, not being sure of facts, and anything that makes life hard for the reader.

☐ **What do you advise writers who want to be published in** *Country Journal* **and comparable publications?**

Be fresh. Give me a new idea. Don't try to reproduce something we've already done. Read the magazine with the goal of figuring out what we want in terms of subject matter, length, tone, and authoritativeness. After you have a sense of the magazine's personality, go to the contents. The categories of coverage will be very similar from one issue to the next. Look at letters to the editor and the back of the book departments. Then come up with a new idea that's a little out of the ordinary.

Think ahead. At *Country Journal* we're seasonal because we are outdoors. If you want to write a spring planting story, give us at least a six-month lead time. Propose your article in the summer, not a month before spring starts.

Don't be afraid to write directly to the editor. You don't have to write to the editorial assistant because you think you're not important.

Don't take it personally if your query is rejected. It could be an absolutely perfect query, but the editor knows that it isn't for his or her magazine. Sometimes the editor can't take the time to explain it in a letter. Don't take it as a personal defeat. It's the idea that's defeated, not you.

Writers should do anything that saves editors work. If you're proposing a piece and you know where photographs could be obtained, whether you take them or not, point that out in the query letter. Editors then won't have to scrounge around for a photographer or an illustrator. Or sketch something out on paper, instead of trying to describe it.

From my standpoint as an editor, a reader is more important than any editor, any advertiser, any printer, or anything. A reader is who I edit for. Although a writer might gear something to an editor to sell a piece, he or she ultimately must write for the reader. And make it one reader, not 300,000. You've got to write for the reader. That's the only person who counts.

20

Writing for *American Baby* and Other Child Care Magazines

JUDITH NOLTE, EDITOR IN CHIEF
American Baby
New York

JUDITH NOLTE obtained undergraduate and graduate degrees in English. She began her publishing career as assistant editor, rising to associate editor at *Bride's* magazine, where she stayed for five years. She moved to *American Baby* in 1969, where she is editor in chief of the child care magazines owned by K-III Magazines Corporation.

American Baby is a free, controlled circulation magazine—it goes to the home on request. *American Baby* is not found on newsstands; the monthly circulation is 1.4 million. The founding date is 1938.

☐ **How do you categorize *American Baby*?**
American Baby is a service magazine primarily directed to expectant and new parents. It offers how-to baby care information and moral support about all those things inexperienced parents worry about when they have a baby.

☐ **Who is your competition?**
Neck on neck, it's a magazine called *Baby Talk*, which is distributed in a similar way, has a comparable circulation, and reaches the same audience (first-time parents of babies up to two years). But we compete for advertising dollars with the bigger magazines that are on the newsstands, such as *Parents*, *Parenting*, and *Child*.

□ Who writes most of your articles?

About 80 percent of the material in the magazine is freelance-written. We assign some articles, but many come in as unrequested queries. We receive about 1,500 unsolicited queries a year. Of those, we publish about 5 percent. We tend to work with a group of writers that we like and trust.

□ Give me examples of typical *American Baby* topics.

We publish on the subjects of safety, baby skin care, crying, sleep problems, all kinds of health problems related to infant care, diapering, dressing, bathing, first-aid, sun care, breastfeeding, bottle-feeding, and nutrition-related issues. We do a lot on day care and child care options, and some financial stories on planning for the new baby. We occasionally talk about the mother's taking care of herself, staying fit, dieting, and losing the weight that she put on during pregnancy. And we do product stories. Those are usually written in-house—new toys, new furnishings, and new clothing for babies.

□ Do your writers need credentials?

It depends on the article. If we're doing an article on prenatal testing, which is very medical, we want a writer who has a scientific background. But if it's a personal experience story, the writer doesn't need to be a professional.

□ Will you read manuscripts submitted over the transom?

Yes. I prefer a manuscript. I can make a decision right then and there. It's either going to be good or it's not going to be good. I used to work almost exclusively with manuscripts. Then the book got bigger and people got more sophisticated. Now they write query letters. When you think about it, a query letter is a two-step process. A manuscript is a one-step process—it's there, you don't have to wait for it to come, you don't have to communicate back and forth about, "Yes, we want it. When are you going to send it?" The manuscript comes in and it's "Take it or leave it."

□ Does a well-written query letter sent over the transom have a chance?

Absolutely. The editorial staff sits down and discusses every query letter that comes in. The best query letters have good writing. A crisp, clear, direct way of saying what the writer is after. Not too cute. Not too gimmicky. Just, "Here's what I want to write about." That's the most important thing. We also want to see clips.

Also, some sense of passion that the writer has and wants to express in this article. I'm not particularly turned on by people who sound like they can do anything you assign them. Much of the material is reader-written by people who have gone through the experience. The tone of the magazine is warm, reassuring, and sounds like it's written by people who have some feeling for parenthood and the experiences that parents go through. I want that to come through in the writing.

□ What's the worst thing an author can do in a query letter?

Submit several ideas that the editor has to respond to individually. I don't like multiple query letters. If a writer has more than one idea in a query, it looks like she is trying to hedge her bets. I would prefer that an author have a sense of importance of one idea and rise or fall on the strength of it rather than sending in six or seven.

□ Are you turned off by a query that is not directed to a specific editor?

No. I don't care who they write it to. Once writers get established with us, they are usually assigned an editor.

□ How long does it take to make a decision after you receive a query?

About six to eight weeks, although we try to get back sooner.

□ What is your pay scale?

We start at about $350 to $400 and occasionally go up to $1,000. We pay $500 to $700 for most of our 1,500-word articles.

□ Do you have pet peeves about writers?

I don't want to have to tell writers why I didn't like their article in person or over the phone. None of us wants to hear from somebody by telephone. I think most sophisticated writers, even if they're beginners, know better than to call an editor. If writers don't know the rules, they learn pretty quickly.

□ What do you advise writers who want to be published in *American Baby*?

They should read the magazine to see what we do. I don't expect them to go back a year or two and look at every issue to know what we've covered. But writers should at least have a sense of the look, the feel, the sound, and the mix of the articles in the magazine.

They must speak in their writing with passion and interest in their subject and seem to know something about it. A good writer, other than having a natural ability with language, must have something to say and a strong feeling for the subject matter. Whether the article is about working out of the home or getting a good day-care person or treating a case of diaper rash, if somebody has been through it and has a strong feel for it, that will come through on the written page.

Writers need to have a real feel for the subject matter. That makes a big difference to us. We're talking about a very important time in a woman's life. The reader wants to know that there's something on those pages that speaks to her in a very personal and emotional way. That must come through in the writing.

We get a little tired of hundreds and hundreds of query letters that come in all the time. But I respect what most writers do. I don't ever want to discourage anybody.

21

Writing for *Seventeen* and Other Young Adult Magazines

JOE BARGMANN, FEATURES EDITOR
Seventeen
New York

JOE BARGMANN is features editor at *Seventeen*. After graduating from college with a journalism degree, Bargmann began his career as a crime reporter for the *Columbia* (Missouri) *Daily Tribune*. He changed gears to become a feature writer, first for *St. Louis* magazine and then for the *Boston Phoenix*. He switched careers one more time and began editorial work at *Seventeen*. Bargmann has held his present position since 1992.

Seventeen magazine, founded in 1944, was the first teen magazine to offer advice and articles about teenagers, as well as "matters of style." According to Bargmann, the term "teenager" didn't exist until after World War II. The whole teenage concept didn't come into full bloom until the 1950s. The release of the movie *Rebel Without a Cause* was the landmark for teenagers.

Most women between the ages of thirteen and sixty read or once read *Seventeen*. "It's their bible," says Bargmann. *Seventeen*'s present monthly circulation is 1.9 million, "and growing," adds Bargmann.

□ **What is *Seventeen*'s competition, and what makes *Seventeen* unique?**
YM (*Young Modern*) is our biggest competitor in terms of circulation. If you compare teen magazines to a slightly older market, you might compare YM to *Cosmo* and *Seventeen* to *Vogue*, *Mademoiselle*, or *Allure*.

Seventeen does two things that set us apart from our competition. Number one is fiction. We're the only mass-market magazine that publishes literary fiction. I look for adult fiction that has teenage protagonists and characters. We also do very serious investigative stories three or four times a year—narratives that can be up to five thousand words long. No other magazine for teenage girls does that.

□ **How do you and your editors gain an understanding of today's teenagers?**

Every one of *Seventeen*'s editors is aware of what's going on in the news, of course, and teenagers are in the news now more than ever. One reason is violence. There are also questions about teenage sexuality that have never existed before. A teenager's position in the family is unique now; given the number of families that are breaking up and the recombinations with intermarriages, remarriages, and stepfamilies, it's a wild time to be a teenager.

□ **Choosing articles for impressionable teenagers is a big responsibility. How does that affect *Seventeen*'s editorial decisions?**

It's a huge responsibility. We know that the girls take to heart whatever they read in the magazine. They tend to take things literally.

Our readers are very proprietary. It is *their* magazine. They own it. We constantly try to figure out ways to respond to them and do what they want. That is how we make editorial decisions. Many magazines are led by what the editors think and feel as individuals, but here it's implicit that the readers rule.

□ **How do you determine teenage reading interests?**

One way is by communicating with our readers. We receive over seven thousand pieces of mail every month, including responses to stories and questionnaires and E-mail. One of our editors does nothing but read and respond to this mail. Her sole purpose is to monitor the feedback from our readers. Every *Seventeen* editor is given a monthly memo about stories that the girls are responding to and what they're saying.

□ **How do you usually acquire articles? Do your editors have a cadre of freelance writers on whom they depend?**

We have a couple of contributing editors. Individual editors also bring in and develop freelance writers. It behooves editors to have a regular association with a group of writers who will deliver the kind of stories that we're looking for. Fifty percent of our articles are freelance-written.

□ **Do you read every query and manuscript?**

We look at all queries and unsolicited manuscripts and consider them on their merit.

□ **What should a good, professional query include?**

I want a well-written, one-page query. Two pages are fine if the writer needs to tell that much of the story to hook me. I certainly hope that the writing in the query is as good as the author can deliver.

A query that has the whiff of being a form letter turns me off immediately. Writers should spell my name correctly, of course. They should demonstrate some familiarity with the magazine—by mentioning an article that has run recently, for instance, or referring to a particular section of the magazine where they think their story might fit.

I look for an original idea or a fresh take on an old idea. I don't want a blunt-edged query about, say, dating violence among teenagers. Everybody knows that story exists. I want to know what you can bring to the subject. Do you have a particular instance to report? Is a girl willing to talk to you in-depth about her experience? How well can you document it?

I want to see three of the writer's best clips. A good idea is not enough. I need to see that the writer can execute.

□ **How long does it take you to decide on a query?**

It varies. It can happen literally in days or it can take up to six months. I just got a great query. We moved quickly because it was timely. On the other hand, if an idea comes to me that is good but needs work, and I think the writer shows promise, I will go through revisions to get that query up to speed before I pitch it upstairs.

□ **What do you look for in clips?**

I look at writing ability on an equal plane with reporting ability. Too many writers think they can get away without much reporting or with just a couple of interviews for an article if their writing is good. That's wrong. The more reporting you do, the easier it is to write a compelling article.

You needn't send an actual tear sheet, but give me a good, clear photocopy. Editors read for ten to twelve hours a day. Struggling through a blurry photocopy is not a joy. In fact, most often I won't do it.

□ **Give me examples of typical *Seventeen* articles.**

Boyfriend-type and relationship pieces are very important. We may do a story about how to break up with a boyfriend or how to fight with a boyfriend. Quizzes are a mainstay. We try to run two quizzes each month. Examples are, "Is he playing you like a cheap fiddle? How assertive are you? How should you deal with criticism?"—nitty-gritty things about relationships or readers' personal lives.

One article in each issue is topical and extremely well reported. For example, a writer from the *Los Angeles Times* is working on a story for us about a girl from Wayne, New Jersey, who flipped a jeep in which two of her friends died. It was a freak accident. How does this event affect the lives of not only the girl who was driving but everyone around her—her parents, her schoolmates, the community?

Another example is a profile we did of a girl who, during her four years of high school, attended forty funerals. This was a great story, a really interesting story about street violence and how it affects teenagers, through one girl's eyes. That, to me, was a home run—it did everything that a *Seventeen* story should do. It was in the news [at the time of publication], but it was a fresh approach. It was engaging because our readers could relate to the girl and it wasn't a complete downer. The message was that she's surviving and, in fact, thriving. How does she do it? What is her life like now? That was an extremely successful story.

□ How can writers determine if they have a great article idea for *Seventeen*?

Read the magazine. That's very basic advice that a lot of writers unfortunately ignore. It's offensive to editors when freelancers ignore that first step. The magazine equals our lives. If you don't pay attention to that advice, if you don't know anything about the magazine, how can you honestly say you want to publish your work there?

□ How do you work with a writer whose "interesting" query needs work?

I call or write and tell the author that the idea is good, but here's where I think it could be stronger, here's what I'd like. I reconsider the idea after the writer revises the query. Most freelancers appreciate the personal attention and make the changes. I offer them no guarantees. I tell them that I personally like the idea but I'm not the editor in chief. I must sell ideas to my boss in much the same way the writer is trying to sell the idea to me.

□ Will you look at manuscripts submitted by freelancers?

Yes, but it takes a while for us to respond—sometimes a week, but maybe as long as two or three months. From my point of view, that's reasonable. From the writer's point of view, it might be nuts. There's absolutely no way that I can guarantee a response in under three months.

□ Are phone calls from writers okay?

No. But there are exceptions. I'll take calls from name writers. I know that's discouraging to people who haven't made a name for themselves yet. I'll also answer calls from writers I've had previous contact with or who are referred by another editor or a good friend of mine. Who you know does help.

□ **Do you offer a contract for each article? What's included in the contract?**

Yes. We pay for first-time North American serial rights. We recently added a clause about electronic rights because we're going on-line. The article will be available electronically to anyone who subscribes to the particular on-line service.

□ **What do you generally pay writers?**

Our going rate for nonfiction is a dollar per word. We will go up, depending on the experience of the writer and the quality of the idea. The "Voice" section, written by younger writers, pays less. Fiction is paid on a per-piece basis and ranges from $750 to $3,000, depending on who the writer is and how great the story is.

□ **Do you have pet peeves?**

The phone call is number one. Just because you've got an editor's number doesn't mean you should use it.

Number two is writers who send a postcard or little note saying, "I have this idea, I am writing this article, are you interested?" If I respond to them in the affirmative, they send back a full-length query that says, "Here is the article you requested." Now I didn't really request that. The request did not originate with me. It's disingenuous for people to do that. It bugs me. If someone sends such a note, I throw it out. Just send me the story.

Another annoyance is writers who get indignant when they don't get a timely response. When a writer is late with a story, I don't get indignant until it's really, really late. I understand what it's like to be busy. Writers must understand that at any given time I may have a dozen stories that I am working on—features that are between two thousand and five thousand words. I am beholden to those writers first. In addition to my fiction and features duties, I am in charge of "Eat," our food section. That gives you an idea of the volume of work that I am personally responsible for. I'm not complaining. I love it. That's just the reality.

A last peeve is when I've said "no," I'll get a note from a writer asking me to reconsider, as if I didn't know what I was doing when I said no. I don't appreciate that.

□ **What should writers do to avoid problems?**

Number one—stay in communication. You've got to tell your editor what's going on. Many writers retreat, withdraw, and don't communicate when the deadline approaches. That's bad. We editors are always being asked by our bosses what's going on with a particular story, and we must have answers. If the writer doesn't provide them, it makes us look bad. So, once you've got an assignment, stay in touch with your editor. If the editor calls you, please return the call.

□ **What do you advise writers who want to be published in *Seventeen* and want to build a career writing for *Seventeen*?**

It's such common sense, it almost sounds stupid. Report the story well. Follow through on everything you agreed to do in terms of the article. Demonstrate that you did a boatload of reporting. That's most important.

Don't hand in a manuscript that's two thousand words longer than the agreed-upon length. Five hundred or in some cases one thousand words over the assigned length is fine with me. It's easier to cut than it is to add. Stories that are longer than that show a lack of control on the writer's part.

Meet the deadline. If you don't meet the deadline, have a good reason why you're not.

Follow through and keep in touch while you're writing the article.

Afterwards, don't become a stranger. Many writers will get an article published in *Seventeen* and nothing will come after that. It's mystifying to me, especially if the article is successful. Writers will know if it was successful or not. I personally get in touch with writers after their article appears and tell them how the boss responded and how the readers responded, so that they have an idea of whether they did a great job. I usually won't call with bad news. My silence will sometimes be an indication that we're not interested in doing another article with that person. I'm always open to ideas after a successful article comes out. It would be nice to know that the writer is interested in working with me again. Hopefully, it was a good experience and they will pitch me some more ideas and not go to the competition.

22

Writing for *Writer's Digest*

Writing for Writers

THOMAS CLARK, EDITOR
Writer's Digest
Cincinnati

THOMAS CLARK graduated from college with a bachelor's degree in journalism. He worked for a weekly newspaper for three years before joining the *Writer's Digest* staff as an assistant editor in 1984. He was quickly promoted to managing editor, a position he held for six years. In 1990 he became senior editor. His current title is editor.

Writer's Digest, founded in 1920, has a monthly circulation of 225,000. The readership consists mostly of female beginning writers who are unpublished or published at a beginning level.

☐ **What types of articles do you publish?**
We publish how-to-write articles almost exclusively. Every piece must have an element of how-to in it. The reader of a *Writer's Digest* article should be able to do something better—that might be writing transitions, writing a better query letter, studying a magazine more effectively, or even reading a novel more effectively.

☐ **What percent of *Writer's Digest* articles are freelance-written?**
Ninety-five percent.

☐ **Do you publish material sent over the transom, or do you have a cadre of writers on whom you depend?**
We do a lot of looking over the transom, but I also have a core of people I can turn to when I have an idea. Our writers have had a fair amount of experience in the marketplace. Academic credits are not necessary. Publication credits most defi-

nitely are. My favorite writers are not too far removed from their beginnings—they have achieved a measure of success, but remember what it was like to be where our audience is. They know the craft and they know what they're doing.

□ How much do you pay?
We pay ten cents to thirty cents per word. The more experience, the higher the pay. Someone who has written for us before will be paid the higher rate. We try to stepladder.

□ What do you look for in a query letter?
There are three basic parts of a query: the opening, the sell copy in the middle, and the resume at the end.

I want a good beginning that captures my attention and, in the process, shows me that the writer knows how to begin an article. I want the letter to lay out the article. It should preview the piece and hint at what will be included. Don't tell me that you're going to give me ten tips for writers, tell me what those tips will be, or give me a selection of them. I want to know who the *writer* is.

The winning query is the one that outlines the article sufficiently and in good depth. It convinces me that the writer has a handle on the topic and knows what he's talking about. This person also must have the experience necessary to speak authoritatively. Also, send clips.

Whether a query is accepted or rejected can be an accident of timing. We may reject a perfectly good query because we have recently published the topic or already have it assigned.

□ Will you look at completed manuscripts?
I don't like to. It takes less time to read a one-page query than it does to read a twelve-page manuscript. Also, I can influence the writing of the manuscript if I've seen it at the query stage. If the manuscript is completed, I may see things that should have been done differently and must decide whether it's worth going back to the writer for a rewrite. I often find a general reluctance from writers to rewrite to the depth that we want. Writers often ask, "How much of the manuscript can I salvage rather than starting over?"

□ How long does the query decision process take?
Three to four weeks. It may take longer. We publish fifteen issues a year. Sometimes there's a lot of copy flying around. Queries tend to be the last thing we look at.

□ What do you want from freelance writers?
An understanding of our audience and the way *Writer's Digest* speaks to that audience. A feeling for what readers want from the magazine and how we deliver on that expectation.

Beyond that, I want writers to help me do my job. I want them to answer my questions and do asked-for revisions. We don't send back material willy-nilly. We try to be very specific about what an article needs and how it can be developed. We put a lot of thought into it. I expect the writer to pay attention.

□ Do you have pet peeves?

Basic editing pet peeves. Writers who are careless with grammar and spelling. Clichés and trite expressions. Headlines like "Confessions of the Housewife Writer" or "Confessions of a First-Time Author" are trite and instantly raise a flag in my head that the writer must overcome.

□ Do you mind phone calls from writers?

Yes. I mind them a lot unless I know the writers and have worked with them, and they have something important to say. Don't call and say, "I just put something in the mail for you." That's why you put it in the mail. I'll know you did when I get it. It's not like I'm going to write your name down and three days later say, "Gee, I never got that." The editor will usually give you a clue as to whether he welcomes your phone call. Excessive friendliness on the phone from writers drives me up the wall. I'm really busy. All editors are.

□ What do you advise writers who want to be published in *Writer's Digest?*

If you want to be published in *Writer's Digest*, get the experience that you need to speak to our readers. Remember what it was like to be a beginning writer and communicate that. We're suckers for that. It works every time.

23

Writing for *The Virginia Quarterly Review* and Other Scholarly Publications

STAIGE BLACKFORD, EDITOR IN CHIEF
The Virginia Quarterly Review
Charlottesville

STAIGE BLACKFORD holds two bachelor of arts degrees. He majored in English at the University of Virginia and read history at Oxford University in England. Blackford worked as a newspaper reporter and encyclopedia editor before he was appointed press secretary and speech writer for Linwood Holten, the first Republican governor of Virginia. Blackford, a Democrat, wrote Holten's inaugural address. Blackford has been editor in chief for *The Virginia Quarterly Review* since 1974.

Founded in 1925, *The Virginia Quarterly Review* is a national journal of literature and discussion, covering subjects from astrology to zoology. The circulation is about four thousand.

☐ **What is the purpose of literary and scholarly journals?**
The purpose is fundamentally to underscore a university's intellectual reputation. The University of Virginia was once reputed to be the country club of the South. *The Virginia Quarterly Review* was proof that the university was more than that. Thomas Jefferson, the university's founder, wanted the university to be a "bulwark for the human mind in the Western Hemisphere." *The Virginia Quarterly Review* was one way to show that bulwark.

□ **How do scholarly publications like *The Virginia Quarterly Review* differ from literary journals?**
Scholarly publications run articles that are not literary. A typical issue we recently ran included an article about the pre-Brown South (re the *Brown v. the Board of Education* Supreme Court ruling), a feature comparing a mixed economy and a premarket economy, and a story about patriotism. *The Virginia Quarterly Review* is more like *The American Scholar* or *The Wilson Quarterly* than it is like the *Sewanee Review* or the *Southern Review*, which only run articles pertaining to literature.

□ **Is *The Virginia Quarterly Review* supported by the University of Virginia?**
Yes. Our salaries are paid by the university.

□ **How do you acquire stories and poetry?**
All I do is sit here and wait. They come pouring in. We receive between two thousand and three thousand unsolicited stories a year, and there were about ten thousand poems the last time I looked. I always look at the first page of the slush. If something seems worthwhile, I give it to outside volunteer readers. A very, very small percent get published. I publish four stories an issue, which adds up to sixteen stories a year. Figure it out.

□ **What sparks your interest in a query or a manuscript?**
A previous track record. It helps if someone has been published before.

I keep a keen eye out for anything in fiction that includes natural humor. We get very little humor.

□ **What do you pay writers?**
We pay a dollar per line for poetry. For short stories, we pay $10 per printed page.

□ **Do you offer a contract for each poem or story?**
No. We have the first copyright and if someone wants the rights, we reassign them.

□ **Do you pay kill fees?**
Yes. If I have accepted an article and haven't had the chance to run it, I will give a kill fee.

□ **Why is it so difficult to be published in scholarly journals?**
One problem is the burgeoning Associated Writing Programs. MFA (Master of Fine Arts) programs have sprung up like Topsy. We turn out all of these would-be poets, short story writers, and novelists who then can't get a job. And what

do we do? We create another MFA program. As a result, we've got five hundred different programs.

□ Who are your writers? Where are they from?

Our writers have ranged from Kathryn Ann Porter and Nancy Hale to Eleanor Roosevelt, Ann Beattie, and Robert Penn Warren. They're from all over the country and all over the world. Part of the reason is that we've been here for more than seventy years.

□ Who are your readers?

Our readership ranges from middle age to old age. I and fellow editors worry about the younger people. They want to write for journals, but they don't want to read them. At one point, I started sending a subscription blank out with every writing assignment. Writers want to get published, but they don't want to subscribe to the magazine. They want you to pay them, but they don't want to pay you. It's an ironic situation.

□ How can writers be published?

Write well. That's easier said than done. The art of writing in this country is not exactly at an all-time high.

One of the problems with younger writers is that they want to be instant Hemingways without doing the reading that Hemingway did. I suggest that writers read more. We are living in an era in which reading is a vanishing art.

□ If reading is a vanishing art, how can journals like *The Virginia Quarterly Review* survive?

I don't know how they will last. I think journals are like people—they have a life expectancy. I'd like to see this journal get past its seventy-fifth anniversary.

□ What is the future of scholarly journals?

Every time I'm asked that question I think of a query from the War Office sent to a British colonel on the beaches of Dunkirk at the height of battle during World War II. The officers in the War Office wanted know what was going on. The colonel sent an instant reply: "Situation obscure, but thought to be improving."

24

Writing for the *ABA Journal* and Other Professional Journals

GARY HENGSTLER, EDITOR AND PUBLISHER

ABA Journal

Chicago

GARY HENGSTLER received a journalism degree in 1969. Although he trained for a career in journalism/education, he opted to go directly into newspapers, starting at the Portland, Indiana *Commercial Review* as city editor. Within a year, Hengstler became managing editor. At twenty-one, Hengstler was Indiana's youngest managing editor of a daily newspaper. In 1973 he moved to the Elyria, Ohio *Chronicle Telegram* as news editor. Hengstler started law school in 1979 and practiced law from 1983 to 1985. He joined the *ABA Journal* as news editor in 1986. Hengstler was promoted to editor and publisher in 1989.

The *ABA Journal* was founded in 1915. The first issue went to 9,600 members of the American Bar Association. The *ABA Journal*'s present monthly circulation is 420,000.

☐ **How are trade association journals different from scientific journals?**
Scientific journals are scholastic, serious, formal, footnoted publications. Trade association journals are not. The *Journal of the American Medical Association* (JAMA) and *The New England Journal of Medicine* are typical scientific publications. Articles published in those journals go through extreme peer review and are the defining scholarly research on the latest medical advances.

Some trade association publications publish articles mainly about the officers and meetings with photos of handshakes and plaque presentations. Other trade journals publish articles about the work or profession that caused the organization to be formed and deemphasize internal association activities.

The ABA *Journal* is a hybrid. We are largely independent of our association, editorially. Therefore, we can publish articles that are critical of the legal profession, which is unusual for an association publication.

□ Does the mainstream media get information from trade journals?

I'll bet most reporters in the general media get a lot of their information from association publications and specific trade books because we learn about it first and are closer to the sources. Specialists at daily newspapers, general-circulation magazines, and the electronic media don't have time to stay abreast of everything to the extent that we do.

□ Is the ABA *Journal* similar to commercial publications?

Yes. Because the static look of a stereotypical house organ publication isn't vibrant or inviting, our journal has shifted to a consumer look. It reads and feels just like a general-circulation magazine. Our readers are used to the look and feel of consumer magazines, and that's the standard they measure us by.

□ Give me an example of an ABA *Journal* article that would fit into a general-circulation magazine.

We ran a detailed, investigative story about a black man who was convicted of murder in Oklahoma. This piece not only demonstrated that this man didn't commit the crime, but the article pointed toward the person who was a better suspect, a man who is in a Texas prison but had been in the area at that time. That piece would have been justifiably in the *Wall Street Journal* or *Newsweek* or it could have been the subject of (the television program) "60 Minutes."

□ What are the titles of other typical ABA *Journal* articles?

"The Troubled Justice System—Why It's Not Meeting Expectations"; "Greed, Ignorance, and Overbilling—The Problems of Attorneys Who Are Padding Their Hours"; "Rediscovering the Middle Class—New and Old Ways to Build a Practice That Americans Want"; "The Future of the Profession"; "How Citizens View the Law through OJ—What That Trial Means to the Legal System."

□ Who writes for the ABA *Journal?* How does this differ from other trade publications?

About 50 percent of our editorial content comes from freelancers, many of whom contribute on a regular basis. A few association magazines are staff-written, but most employ professional editors who polish copy that is written by volunteers.

□ Will you publish articles by writers who are not lawyers?

Our writers don't need a law degree, but they should be trained legally. A writer can obtain familiarity with the language, the processes, and the legal system if that's his or her beat. My Washington correspondent doesn't have a law degree, but he covered the Supreme Court for United Press International for several years. If you write for a newspaper and cover the courts or if you cover science or medicine, you can write for corresponding trade journals.

□ Do you get many unsolicited queries?

Yes. We also get a lot of unsolicited manuscripts. Less than 10 percent are published.

□ What sparks your interest in a query letter?

The query should explain not only "what" but how you've done preliminary research. It should show that you're not just shooting from the hip. A writer may have a shot at getting published if he or she has found that little nugget or tie-in that we haven't thought of.

□ How much do you pay for articles?

It depends. We usually pay between $1,500 for a 2,000 to 3,000 word feature article. But these are general guidelines. We will go higher or lower, depending on the quality of the work and the demand for the writer.

□ Do you have pet peeves?

I have problems with freelancers who clearly have never looked at this magazine to see what we've written about in the past. Writers often suggest articles that we published within the past two or three months.

I receive a lot of thoughtless queries. For example, in the wake of the OJ Simpson case, freelancers wrote to me saying, "I'd like to write about OJ." Well, yes. Who wouldn't? It's not as if the largest legal magazine in the world hasn't given some thought about the most high-profile trial in the United States and how we want to cover it. For us to hear from an individual who has no demonstrable track record and who generically says he wants to write about OJ is waste of that person's time and my time.

I get annoyed at freelancers who assume, after receiving a rejection, that we didn't consider their query fully. I suddenly get a call and the writer wants to argue the case. Some of them are not very civil about it. It's like, "How dare you! I'm good. Why can't you recognize it?" Even if I made a mistake and rejected an idea that I probably should have accepted, that approach will not make me go back and think about it again.

□ How should writers approach you if they think that their idea might be reconsidered?

I'll be happy to talk to someone who calls and says, "I understand your rejection, but could you elaborate on it? I don't want to make this mistake with you in the future." We try to make rejections as personal as possible. We don't use generic forms. We try to give some indication of where our thought process was and why the idea didn't meet our needs. When a writer says, "How dare you! This is the greatest thing ever written," it seems that he thinks his journalistic and intellectual ability is superior to ours. There's enough ego in journalism that not all of us are ready to concede that.

□ What do you advise freelancers who want to be published in major trade magazines?

Freelancers should be like the biblical Ruth. Ruth got permission from the owner of a field to pick up the gleanings after the harvesters did their job. Ruth survived by picking up things that the harvesters had missed. The moral to the story is, unless you're a big-name writer who is established with many magazines, you can't demand the center spotlight for a feature article or a major story. Beginning writers should find those odd, tidbit aspects of news, developments, and issues that the editors may not have thought about or may have overlooked. Or, they may have a perspective or access to an angle that we missed.

If you want me to read your query, take the time to look up my name and write to me personally. Little things like "Dear Sir" or "Dear Editor" are turn-offs. I try to respond back to individuals personally. If writers don't like form letter rejections, they ought not send form letter queries.

Be aware of details and proofread your letters. It's amazing how many misspellings and grammar errors we see. The sloppiness in query letters and unsolicited manuscripts sabotages what the writer has to say. Poor technical skills will raise questions about the substantive matter of an article.

Freelancers should get an area of expertise, then study that market and get familiar with the publications they want to target. Always target your article and your audience.

Learn the style and know the feel of the magazines for which you want to write. I receive two-inch-thick manuscripts, usually from lawyers, complete with footnotes and other citations, written in stilted language. The last time these people wrote was probably for a law review, in a detailed scholastic style that rivals *JAMA* on the medical side. If these writers had taken the time to read our magazine—two or three issues would do it—they'd see that we don't use footnotes and that our articles are written in a magazine style. Even if it's the same information that could be published in a law review, these writers must present a more graceful and inviting style.

25

Writing for *Cornell Magazine* and Other College and Alumni Magazines

STEPHEN MADDEN, EDITOR AND PUBLISHER
Cornell Magazine
Ithaca, New York

STEPHEN MADDEN was a published author before he graduated from college. During his junior and senior years, he wrote part-time for the *Cornell Alumni News* and was, at the same time, a reporter for the *Ithaca Journal.* "I spent more time at the magazine and the newspaper than I did at school and I have the grades to prove it," says Madden. After graduation, Madden was hired by *Fortune* magazine as a fact-checker. After six months he was promoted to reporter, then columnist. He moved to M magazine as a staff writer. In 1991 he joined the *Cornell Alumni News* as editor. He quickly climbed the ranks to associate publisher, then editor and publisher.

Cornell Alumni News was founded in 1899 by a group of alumni who wanted to stay in touch with each other. The name was changed to *Cornell Magazine* in 1993. *Cornell Magazine*'s monthly circulation is 40,000.

☐ **What percentage of colleges and universities publish alumni magazines?**
About 99 percent.

□ How are alumni magazines similar and how do they differ?

Some alumni magazines have huge budgets and are amazingly good. Some are dismal. At the top alumni magazines, you get terrific editing. The editors know what they're doing and care about the craft. They also realize that [the magazine is read] by smart people. So they publish more than just trips down memory lane and they're honest with their readers. Dismal alumni magazines insult the readership by telling them nothing but good news about the alma mater. We're all fundraisers. We want to keep alums connected with the university. About 99 percent of colleges and universities publish alumni magazines. Some alumni magazines are 100 percent subsidized, some are zero percent subsidized. We get free rent and office space.

□ Are alumni magazines a good market for freelance writers?

They are a terrific, undertapped market for freelance writers. About 70 percent of the non-class-notes content of our magazine is freelance-written.

□ Are editors of alumni magazines more inclined to publish writers who are graduates or students?

Graduates have a foot in the door. We're more likely to look at their clips. A graduate is more likely to have seen the magazine, which is a help in pitching a story. Students also have a better chance. I'm more patient with student manuscripts because we're at an educational institution. We have a responsibility in that direction. I benefited from editors here when I was a student. For me, it's a karmic debt.

□ Do you have a stable of regular writers?

In 3½ years, more than one hundred people have written for this magazine. About twenty of them write for us regularly. Most of our article ideas are generated in-house. We assign the article to the proper writer to get the proper treatment.

□ What do you look for in a freelance writer?

Someone who is familiar with the magazine. A writer who delivers what we want, what we need when we need it, and who is willing to rewrite for us. We publish profiles of alumni and faculty and issue-oriented articles. There's virtually no issue that's of interest to the world at large that you can't find a Cornellian involved in. We don't do many scholarly pieces.

□ Do you read every query letter and manuscript that comes in over the transom?

I or my staff writer reads everything that comes in. What we like is a query that's hip to the magazine. You've got to pick up on the ethic of the magazine. A query that's well written. Most query letters are flat and formulaic. A query that makes the writer and the topic stand out. A query that's not too up on itself. I don't like letters that say, "I'm sure this will make a valuable contribution." A query that's not acting like it's doing me a huge favor.

□ What do you look for in clips from new writers?

Clips should be interesting, competent, and well reported. I must admit that clips from *New York* magazine will open my eyes quicker than clips from the newsletter of Southern Tier Daughters of the American Revolution. However, if the piece in a lesser-known publication is well written, that's important.

□ Do you offer a contract for every article?

Not for every article. If a writer wants one, we will provide a standard contract.

□ What do you and other alumni magazines pay freelancers?

Cornell Magazine's normal rates are $1,000 for a 2,500-word feature. That's nowhere near national rates, but it's not dog-track money either. Many other alumni magazines also pay well.

□ What endears one writer to you more than another?

We have a very informal operation. I sit here in jeans, boots, and a sweater. I've got my dog with me. I try to create an environment where it's okay for people to say what's on their mind because that's going to aid the creative process. The magazine ultimately benefits. I like a writer who can pick up on that, who's not a stiff.

□ Do you have pet peeves?

I hate surprises. I hate someone who says. "I'll do a 3,000-word profile" and it comes in at eight thousand words. That's not a profile, it's a polemic. That person won't work for us again. My other pet peeves are writers who take short cuts and don't report thoroughly, slipshod writing, misspellings in query letters, especially my first name, which is often misspelled. It's in print all over the magazine. It's not that hard to check.

□ What do you advise writers who want to be published in alumni magazines?

Care about what you're doing. Let me tell you what's probably an apocryphal story. Henry Kissinger gave his research assistant a project. After she submitted it, he called her into his office. "Is this the best you can do?" he asked. "No, I guess not," she answered. She took the work back to do more research and writing. This process was repeated several times. She finally came back and handed him the report. "Is this the best you can do?" he asked her. "Yes, this is the best I can do," she answered. Kissinger then said, "Okay, now I'll read it."

That's how I feel. I'm not adverse to giving guidance and making suggestions, but I often feel that on first blush I'm not getting the author's best work.

If you're going to take my money, you ought to do your best. This can be a fairly lucrative market. A lot of alumni magazine editors are looking for writers. I'm looking for writers who give a damn about their work and my publication. I wake up in the middle of the night worrying about the magazine. I appreciate it when writers feel the same about their work—when they are passionate and concerned with their writing.

26

Writing for *Popular Science* and Other Scientific Magazines

FRED ABATEMARCO, EDITOR IN CHIEF
Popular Science
New York

FRED ABATEMARCO, editor in chief of *Popular Science*, was bitten by the publishing bug as a college undergraduate. A part-time job at the *Wall Street Journal* during his junior and senior years spurred his interest in business journalism. After graduation, Abatemarco cut his teeth in New York City at WCBS news radio. He began to cover technology at the *Elmira Star Gazette* and at Fairchild Publications. He moved to *Newsweek* magazine as an associate editor for their international edition, where technology remained his beat. He then joined *Personal Computing Magazine* and rapidly rose from assistant managing editor to editor in chief. Abatemarco has been editor in chief of *Popular Science* magazine since 1989.

Founded in 1872, *Popular Science* is the fifth-oldest continuously published magazine and the largest science and technology magazine in the United States, with a circulation of 1.8 million. The magazine was started in the midst of the Industrial Revolution when the fruits of scientific discoveries were significantly affecting people's lives but the general public had little knowledge of what was happening in laboratories. *Popular Science Monthly*, the magazine's original title, was based on the premise that everyday citizens would be better off knowing what scientists and engineers were working on.

Popular Science's monthly circulation is nearly 2 million.

□ What publications are comparable to *Popular Science?*

Scientific American, *Discover*, *Omni*, and *Popular Mechanics*. That's generally considered the science/technology field.

□ How does *Popular Science* stand out from the competition?

Popular Science is the journal of fast-moving, hard, shiny objects. We try to be a window on the world of technology—what's new, what's coming, and how it will affect our lives. *Scientific American* is a much more theoretical magazine for professional scientists. *Discover* was modeled as a weekly news magazine of science. *Omni* is dedicated to a borderline area where science fiction meets science reality. *Popular Mechanics* is a "do-it-yourself around the house" kind of magazine.

□ What is the meat of *Popular Science* and what are typical articles?

The "What's New" section is the hallmark of the magazine. It is graphically and photographically rich with examples and brief explanations of new technology.

Feature articles describe the people and events that stand behind [technological] developments and the ramifications thereof. For example, we did a cover story on the collision of asteroids with Jupiter. We talked about how such a discovery was made, the scientists who made it, and the ramifications.

It's the background, the event, and the "what does this mean to me" angle that is typical of a major article.

□ How do you decide which articles to publish?

That's a tough question because there's so much going on in the field. As a monthly magazine we've got to make hard choices. There's a whole philosophy in terms of what we cover and how we cover it. I always try to keep it tracked to the effect on people's lives—what is significant and what will make the most interesting reading? We also try to look at the impact. If a new computer chip is developed, will this impact people personally, communally, or globally? We use that as a gauge to help us plan our coverage and decide what goes into an issue. I have nearly 2 million readers to serve. I am competing for their attention more so than ever before.

□ How do you usually acquire articles?

The magazine is half staff-written and half freelance-written. Fifty percent of the freelance articles are provided by contributors whom we work with on a regular basis. About 25 percent of articles make their way to us based on queries that we review and assign.

□ Who are the writers you work with on a regular basis? Do they have credentials?

They are mostly proven journalists. They're usually writers and not scientists. Journalistic expertise and credentials are much more important to us than the scientific ones. It never hurts and it works out that many of the people we work with have some kind of scientific training, education, or experience. But that's not a rule by any means.

□ How can a first-time author break in at *Popular Science* and what does that lead to?

When somebody puts together an interesting query and piques our interest in a noteworthy event, we're very willing to publish a first-time writer in our news-front section, where we run quite a few short articles. Even if we haven't worked with her or she may not have a clip file as long as your arm, we're willing to take a shot with somebody like that on a short piece, if that query gives us a sense that she's probably pretty good. We can then gain experience working with this writer, which often leads to larger articles.

□ What constitutes a good, professional query letter?

The query letter has to be short and to the point. There's a ton of material that crosses every editor's desk that he'll never get to. The bread and butter of what we do is tracking down ideas and creating journalism. We need to see and grasp it quickly. There's got to be a very brief communication as to what the story is and why I should care as an editor. In other words, why should my magazine publish this and why would my readers care? I'm my readers' agent. I'm my readers' filter. The writer has an obligation to communicate as quickly, efficiently, and as powerfully as possible. If a writer does that, I have the first bit of confidence that he or she is going to use that kind of power communication in the writing.

Next, I want to know what qualifies this writer to do the story. After a writer convinces me that I care about a particular story, the most important credential is access that no one else has. He's already done the research, he's had a key interview, he's witnessed an event and/or has access to an upcoming event—that is a major resource to me.

□ Do you always want to see clips from a first-time writer, and what do you look for in them?

Yes. I look for signs of good writing. A writer's ability to express complex ideas in a clear and understandable way is very important in science writing. I also look for an interesting writing style. If I see those items, I have a level of confidence to go forward and talk to the writer and try to develop the story. A potential pitfall in science writing is that the story can be deadly dull if handled wrong. I'm always looking for somebody's ability to story-tell. The most important thing in magazine journalism and all media is to tell people stories.

□ Would you rather receive a query than a completed manuscript?

I'd much rather see a query. Even if you have a completed manuscript, I'd rather you send me the query. The manuscript will be put on the low part of my work pile. We're going to look at queries first. We'll look at the manuscripts when we get a chance. There's a very good chance that you may not have done this manuscript just the way the editor likes. And we're going to stop reading it. As soon as we stop reading it, it's going to the "thanks, but no thanks" pile. If you send the query and we follow up on the query, we're more likely to endure the weaknesses of that manuscript and continue to work with you to shape it. It's just like looking for a job. As soon as you turn that editor off, you've lost your chance. Not forever. But for that one instance. So give editors as little as possible to turn them off. Give them only what is required.

□ **How long does it take you to decide on a query that has sparked your interest?**

There's no set answer. It can be something that needs to be kicked around internally for a couple weeks or it can get an immediate response in less than a week. It depends on what significance the magazine places on the query and the particular editor whose desk it drops on. Every editor has a different style. Submissions can go up the chain, they can go down the chain, they can land in the middle and go both ways. They can go around in circles for a while. At my magazine it works all different ways. A lot of people will blindly send me queries and they will reach my desk. I will send them down the chain. Lots of queries are sent to the associate editor. They will then work their way up the chain.

□ **How much do you pay freelancers and on what do you base the pay?**

We pay about a dollar per word. It has less to do with the writer's experience than it does with the complexity of the story. The asterisk on that answer is that I'm going to have to pay John McPhee more money to do an article about the Chaparral forest than I am a beginning writer. That's just the way it is. But a dollar per word is our standard fee. If a story is less complex, we'll negotiate down; if it's more complex, we'll negotiate up.

□ **Do you offer contracts and kill fees for each article?**

Yes. We offer 25 percent kill fees.

□ **Do you have pet peeves about writers?**

The two things that drive me crazy are writers who don't deliver when they say they will and writers who deliver stories that are not what was discussed. Those two things must be adhered to. If you say you're going to deliver the story in a month, deliver the story in a month. If you're not happy with the story, you need to communicate that. I like to make sure that a story, not just a subject or an event, is agreed upon up front. Writers who don't deliver the story that was agreed upon but something else show a tremendous lapse of communication. From the time a story is assigned to the time the reporting is finished and the research is done and the writing actually takes place, an enormous amount of things change. It's the writer's responsibility to communicate those changes. For example, the writer might say, "By the way, the story we are working on has taken an interesting turn based on this interview and I think you ought to know about it and we should go in this direction." I want to hear communication like that. I do not like surprises.

Here's a big mistake that some writers make regarding science writing. They think that it's science/technical writing or they think that it's science writing. We do *science writing*. Fundamentally that's journalism. The subject happens to be science. Technical writing is what professionals in the fields of engineering or science or some specialty need to get data or information that they can act on. Scientific writing is also very specialized for a very specialized audience. It does not qualify as journalism. We're trying to inform our public. We're not delivering data in a dry way.

□ **What do you advise writers who want to write for** *Popular Science* **or comparable publications?**
My advice to writers is write it like a writer but research it like a scientist. Fact-check it like a scientist, but write it like a writer. You have to keep in mind the fundamental and important aspects of good magazine writing—clarity, accessibility of information and material to the reader, and above all, interest.

Science is this great process of discovery. Scientists try to unveil a mystery— they observe the world and try to figure out what's going on. It's an ongoing process. That situation or event is ripe for great storytelling. As a journalist, you are the eyes and ears of the people who aren't there. You absorb all of the detail of the who, the where, the why, and so on. These are great dramatic elements of storytelling. It's much different than looking at a potato and saying, "What am I going to write about this potato? This potato isn't doing anything."

27

Writing for *Arthritis Today* and Other Health-Issues Magazines

CINDY McDANIEL, EDITOR
Arthritis Today
Atlanta

CINDY McDANIEL holds an undergraduate degree in public relations/journalism and a master's degree in marketing. She initially worked in publications and marketing with a large medical center before joining the Arthritis Foundation. McDaniel soon became involved with the launch of *Arthritis Today*. She has been editor of the magazine since its founding in 1987.

Published six times a year, *Arthritis Today* is a membership benefit of the Arthritis Foundation. Its circulation is about 600,000.

☐ **How do you categorize *Arthritis Today*?**
Arthritis Today doesn't fall neatly into any one category, but we consider it a health publication. It's mainly for people with arthritis, their family members, and the health professionals who care for them. The average age of our readers is around sixty because arthritis is primarily a disease of older people, but we also have many younger readers and we work to keep our content relevant to them as well. It could also be categorized as a magazine for people with disabilities because many people with arthritis have significant physical limitations. But our editorial doesn't focus on disability.

☐ **How do you come up with article ideas?**
About forty percent to fifty percent of our articles are staff-generated and then assigned to freelancers. The other fifty percent to sixty percent come from freelancers—usually established writers who know what we're looking for. If an

idea that we love is submitted from someone we've never heard of, we may buy it.

❑ **If someone whom you haven't previously worked with offers you a great article idea, will you let him or her have a first shot at writing it?**
Yes, but that's not automatic. We probably would make the assignment to a writer who has very strong writing credentials, who has been published repeatedly in respected magazines that we're familiar with, and who sends us good clips that show quality and depth of writing.

❑ **What will help beginning writers get published in your magazine?**
We don't require formal credentials, but it's important that a writer has experience and knowledge of medical topics. Writers should show us that they can talk to researchers and understand technical information. Writers who have a personal relationship with arthritis—if they or a family member have the disease—have a bonus when we decide whether to work with a writer. That personal connection gives them empathy for our readers. Writers who ask for background information about arthritis will rank higher because of their willingness to learn.

❑ **Once a freelancer breaks in, will he or she become part of your pool of regular contributors?**
A published article doesn't necessarily mean that the writer will be a regular contributor. Many one-time writers looked great on paper, but things happened that made us unwilling to work with them again. Their article may have been sub-par or they may have been difficult to work with.

❑ **How many query letters do you receive and, of those, how many get published?**
We receive at least a thousand query letters a year. Of those, we buy about ten or twelve feature articles. It's tough to find writers who stand out from the crowd.

❑ **What happens to a query after it comes in?**
Our associate editor receives all queries. She immediately rejects those that are inappropriate for our magazine, or contain a lot of misspellings and grammatical errors, or include politically incorrect language. In our field, writers must be careful about how they state certain things. This is where disability issues come in. A writer who shows a total lack of sensitivity will get a straightforward rejection.

If the query was not rejected and returned, the associate editor sends it to one of our senior editors. If she likes the query, we communicate with the writer and say, "We really like your idea. We'd like to know more about it." If the idea is really terrific, we may buy it immediately and work it into the next issue, but that's very rare. It usually takes longer to get a yes decision than a no decision.

□ **What is your definition of a good query letter?**

A good query has a clear explanation of the topic without a lot of extra words. The best query letters are often just a paragraph or two that clearly states the topic. The query must demonstrate the writer's knowledge of the subject. Sources of information should be listed. The query should make the editors feel confident that the writer has given enough thought to the article, that there is a story, and that the writer knows how to get the information.

□ **What do you look for in clips?**

The main thing we look for is the writing style. Then we look at the depth of coverage—what kind of research went into the article, its pertinence, and how it might relate to a topic that we might cover.

□ **What types of articles do you publish? What is your slant?**

We've done articles on the ADA (Americans with Disabilities Act). We focus on concepts for better living with arthritis—emotional and physical. We talk about ways that people with mobility limitations due to arthritis can adapt to various activities such as gardening and driving.

We usually publish an inspirational/emotional coping article in each issue. We also include exercise articles (ways to modify exercise for people with arthritis) and medical pieces (overviews of arthritis, updates on medications, information about surgery). Cover stories are usually an arthritis angle on a current newsworthy topic or an in-depth service piece, perhaps with a slightly alternative viewpoint.

□ **How can writers who want to be published in special health publications learn about politically correct language?**

That information is usually covered in the magazine's writer's guidelines. Freelancers can obtain our writer's guidelines and a free copy of the magazine simply by asking. Since we're not a newsstand publication, writers should send for a copy of our magazine and study it to get a feel for the tone, the topics, and the language.

□ **How much do you pay freelance writers?**

We pay between $500 and $1,500, depending on the length of the article, the amount of research needed, and the writer's experience, among other factors.

□ **What are your pet peeves?**

One pet peeve is sloppy query letters that include misspellings, grammatical errors, and/or politically incorrect language. It's not that difficult with today's technology to make a query letter look nice. Another problem is queries without adequate information. We occasionally get query letters from writers that have no phone number. That amazes me. Once an assignment is under way, another pet peeve is writers who disappear, who are out of touch when we try to contact them. In cases like that, the chances are that the articles will not be submitted as we would like to see them. Another pet peeve is writers who are defensive or resist making changes to meet our needs and standards.

□ Describe writers who endear themselves to you.

Writers who request information from us on our topic, who work diligently to get sources and check with us about them, who double-check information, who handle problems along the way, and who stay in close contact with us during an assignment.

□ What do you advise writers who want to be published in *Arthritis Today* and comparable publications?

Learn about the magazine. Show us your knowledge. At *Arthritis Today*, we don't ask you to be an expert on arthritis, but you must have knowledge of the field and of the topics that you're covering.

Make your query letter as appealing and as easy to read as possible. Hone in on the target. Target your letter, target your contacts. Learn as much as you can about the publication that you're targeting and let the editors know that you've done your research. Writers who submit queries that are obviously not tailored to our magazine waste their time and ours.

Once you've been given an assignment, be sure you understand what the editor wants. Ask a lot of questions when you're discussing the article. Call the editor when you're doing the research. Check in regularly to be sure that what you're getting and what you're doing is on target.

28

Writing for *Fitness* and Other Fitness and Health Magazines

JENNIFER COOK, EXECUTIVE EDITOR
Fitness
New York

JENNIFER COOK majored in English literature and modern dance in college, though her first job after graduation was with three industrial relations journals in London. After she returned to the United States, Cook worked her way up the magazine publishing ladder from fact-checker at *New York* magazine, copyeditor at *Working Woman*, and junior writer at *Self*, to managing editor at *Health*, articles editor at *Glamour*, and executive editor at *Fitness*. Cook joined *Fitness* in February 1995.

Fitness was founded in 1987 as part of *Family Circle*'s Special Interest Publishing series. In 1992 *Fitness* became a quarterly, and in 1993 it went bimonthly. By 1995 it was (and still is) published ten times a year. *Fitness*'s circulation is about 700,000.

☐ **How do you categorize *Fitness*?**
Fitness is a women's service magazine. A caption under the logo reads "mind, body, spirit." Our conception of fitness is larger than just exercise—it's a comprehensive way of looking at health and well-being. Fitness touches upon a woman's life in many areas—diet, exercise, health, preventive health, spirituality, and sexuality. *Fitness* falls somewhere between *Self* and *Shape*. *Self* is more like other women's magazines, with stories on beauty, the environment, and the like, plus fitness, whereas *Shape* is more exercise-oriented and preaches to the converted. Our readers are mostly in their twenties, thirties, and forties—the median age is thirty-one—but they range from teenagers to women in their

seventies. They participate in exercise programs, take care of their bodies, and eat right. Or they may have a beginning interest in fitness and might be inspired to change their bodies and/or their outlook.

□ How much of *Fitness* is freelance-written?

About three-quarters is freelance-written. We choose from a stable of contributing editors, regular contributors, and other freelancers. Some began writing for us when they sent a query letter that we liked and we assigned them the story.

□ Is *Fitness* a good market for first-time writers to break in at?

It's an okay market, depending on the kind of story the freelancer wants to write. First-time writers can write first-person stories, which could be exercise experiences or aspects of fitness that touched their lives.

□ What topics are not assigned to a first-time writer?

We're not likely to assign a health piece that requires heavy research to a beginning writer. Writers who don't know the field can't package the story appropriately. Ideas proposed by beginners are usually not right for us.

□ What do you look for in a writer?

We want writers who have covered medicine and health for several years, who follow trends and news in the field of medicine, and who can get to the right sources. These writers often attend medical society meetings to stay abreast of the latest medical news.

□ Are you saying that your writers or those who want to write on medical issues must make health and medicine their beat?

Yes. A writer has too much responsibility not to. If you're writing health and medicine articles for 2 million people, you must develop a background. You can't expect to wade in and write off the top of your head. Our fact-checking department contacts doctors or other sources and goes over quotes, information, and theories.

□ When a writer with a background in health and medicine queries you for the first time, do you want to see clips?

Yes, but I want no more than three or four clips. I don't want to be overwhelmed with too much material. I want to see the writer's best work that relates to areas in which I'll be assigning. I'm looking for creativity in the writing style—the lead and how quickly it draws me in. I want to see that the organization and structure of the stories make sense. The subjects must be newsworthy.

□ What areas should freelancers query you on?

Our stories are very topical and news-oriented. We publish preventive rather than treatment-oriented health stories. You're not likely to see an in-depth story on heart disease drugs for women in our magazine.

Since we are a service magazine, we run many of the same topics over and over again. Freelancers should present a new hook that will make their story fresh and slightly different from those previously published. Writers can query us in the areas of fitness, diet and nutrition, health, adventure fitness, and sex and sensuality.

□ What is your definition of a good, professional query?

A query not only sells the idea but it also sells the writer as the perfect person to write the story. I want to see writing flair in the query letter and, depending on the topic, an engaging or funny turn of phrase. The query letter should state the writer's qualifications and background. I want details of the subject that will convince me of the writer's grasp of the topic. Studies or specific sources should be listed. It's also nice when a writer suggests a title. It shows the writer's creativity and that he or she is trying to be helpful. A title also helps focus the story. That can be useful to the writer and the editor.

□ Will you look at completed manuscripts?

I prefer query letters but I don't mind completed manuscripts from first-time writers because it's hard to get in the door and they probably don't have clips. The manuscript should be no longer than two thousand words.

I'm usually less open to receiving a completed manuscript from an experienced writer. Often, those writers have sent the story to ten other editors. I don't feel that I'm being spoken to as an individual editor. Except for personal essays, a completed story usually has to be rewritten or redirected for my magazine.

□ Is it okay for writers to call about a story idea?

I'd rather get a query than a call about a story. It's okay for writers to call to check on their query after four to six weeks.

□ How much do you pay freelancers?

The going rate is a dollar per word. It may be more for an experienced writer or an in-depth piece or if we're asking for it very quickly. In time, the fee may increase if a writer contributes on a regular basis. We cover expenses like photocopying, Federal Express, phone calls, and so on. Writers should ask about expenses up front, especially if a trip is involved or they plan to call Hong Kong twenty-five times at odd hours and run up a big phone bill.

□ Do you offer contracts for every article?

We offer contracts for everything that we publish.

□ What are your kill fees?

We pay 20 percent kill fees.

□ Do you have pet peeves about things writers do?

One pet peeve is calls from writers I don't know who say, "I'm going to this meeting. Do you want me to do something for you?" I can't deal with that. I need an idea, or I need to know the writer. Another pet peeve is writers who won't take no for an answer, who call repeatedly after I reject a query. If it's a writer I don't know, I would find it hard to work with that writer again.

□ Do you have advice to writers who want to be published in *Fitness* or health sections of other major magazines?

Despite what I said about writers who won't take no for an answer, I believe that people should not give up. Perseverance will take you places. Perseverance and focusing your craft to become a better writer are critical to getting published and staying published.

29

Writing for *Penthouse* and Comparable Magazines

PETER BLOCH, EDITOR
Penthouse
New York

PETER BLOCH's college major was English. After graduation and two years in the army (he was drafted), he worked as a computer programmer for a life insurance company. "I hated it," says Bloch. "One day I walked into the *New York Times* and said, 'I'll take any job as long as it has something to do with newspapers.'" Bloch became a news assistant for the *New York Times* news service. Two years later, he went to *Penthouse* as a copyeditor. He ultimately became editor.

Penthouse was founded in the United States in 1969 by Robert Guccione. The present monthly circulation is 1.2 million to 1.3 million. "The circulation fluctuates because we are about 75 percent newsstand-driven," explains Bloch. "Our circulation depends on a lot of things—like the weather, the economy, or the contents of a particular issue."

□ **How do you categorize *Penthouse?***
Penthouse is a sexually oriented men's magazine that features entertainment and information. The pictures and Forum letters are the main reason that most people buy the magazine. But it is a package. Our readers are mostly men, but also more women than one might think. We get a lot of mail from women who are girlfriends, wives, or friends of men who buy the magazine.

□ What is the socioeconomic status of your readers?

That's a very good question and it's one that defines why my job is both exasperating but also very interesting. There's no way to define *Penthouse* readers in one sentence. Our readers are everyone from Wall Street executives, Washington politicians, and people in the Pentagon and the CIA, to blue-collar workers, people in the armed forces, truck drivers, prisoners, and college students.

They cover the entire country. We sell more copies in urban areas than nonurban areas. But we have many readers in middle-America, in suburban and outlying areas. Our articles must appeal to all these people.

□ Why is there a *Penthouse* niche?

Men like to look at beautiful women. More than that, they obviously like the package that we give them. I can say that with certainty because we also put out five or six publications each month that *only* have girls and sexy letters. They're called *Girls of Penthouse, Penthouse Letters*—a whole bunch of titles that only include the sexual elements. They're a couple of dollars cheaper than *Penthouse* yet they sell only a small percentage of what *Penthouse* sells. The people who buy *Penthouse* are obviously looking for more than just the girls.

□ Which magazine is your closest competitor?

Playboy, our closest competitor, has a huge editorial staff and likes to get big-name writers and big-name book excerpts that they can splash on the cover. We are a lot sexier and, in our investigative articles, we take a lot more chances.

□ How does *Penthouse* compare to magazines that aren't as sexually explicit, such as *Esquire* or *GQ*?

Esquire and GQ are trying to be as sexually explicit as they can. *Esquire* probably runs more articles about sex than we do. GQ is a fashion magazine but it sometimes has naked women in its fashion spreads. *Esquire* and GQ readers are mainly urban, upscale men. Their articles are of interest to that small, affluent group. Remember, we sell to truck drivers and blue-collar people as well as well-heeled lawyers. We must have a broader base.

□ Tell me about the articles that you publish.

We like to take a different view of things. We like to be controversial. We like to mix it up. We're best known for investigative reporting—the cutting-edge journalism that we've made our name on. We thrive on exposés. And we do profiles of people who are popular with our audience. One article explored false allegations of child abuse, a problem that is becoming prominent in courts, usually in divorce cases, where men are falsely accused of abusing children. The Paula Jones story (the woman who accused President Clinton of sexual improprieties) was another typical exposé. We did profiles of radio talk show hosts Howard Stern and Don Imus. We gave some insight on what makes them tick.

□ How do you usually acquire articles?
We come up with one-third of the article ideas and assign them. The other two-thirds come in from writers and agents or are book excerpts.

□ What percentage of your feature articles are written by freelance writers?
Almost 100 percent.

□ Does everything that comes in over the transom get read?
Yes. Somebody looks at everything.

□ Does a writer who has never been published in a major magazine have a chance at *Penthouse*?
Yes. We have published articles by people who have just sent queries or manuscripts in and who have not been published elsewhere. But it's a long shot. *Penthouse* looks like a big magazine, but when you take away the pictorials, the ads, the cartoons, and the regular features, we publish a limited number of articles each month. Most of the permanent features, like the book reviews and the movie reviews, are written by regular writers.

□ How can a first-time writer spark your interest?
The writer must offer something special. We don't want another profile of someone who has been profiled to death in the national media or another article on a topic that everyone else is writing about. Every time there's a plane crash, I get dozens of queries from people who want to write about airline safety. We can't repeat material that has been in *Time* magazine two or three months before.

Along with that, a writer must ask himself, "What do I know or have that makes my insight and information unique?" If you don't have something special, don't query me.

That goes for very experienced writers as well as first-time writers. I don't care if you've written twenty books. If you're sending me a query about something old, it won't be bought.

□ How much do you pay writers?
We pay $3,000 and up for a major feature. It depends on the amount of time needed, the subject, and the writer. We will pay more to writers we have worked with many times before or big-name writers, whose names will help sell more copies.

□ Do you have pet peeves about writers?

Phone calls from writers who don't have a good reason or who don't know me. I hate phone calls from "crafty" writers who pretend it's personal. Don't tell my secretary that you're a friend, when you're not. People do that a lot. That's a good way to never get an assignment.

I don't like to be oversold on an idea or an article. If you send a query that says, "This is the hottest story, the biggest exposé," and it isn't—it's just some lame recap of something—you're going to lose total credibility with me and you won't get any further.

Faxes. Unless it's a cutting-edge story, I hate to have my fax machine tied up by writers I never heard of sending me endless blabber.

□ What should writers do to be published in *Penthouse?*

If you have an entire article, send it in. I'd rather read the article. That tells me everything. A lot of writers write great query letters but poor articles.

A query should be a couple of pages long, indicating what will make this article special. Send clips that give a sense of what you want to do for *Penthouse*, what you're like as a writer. Don't send me thousands of clips. Nor do I want to see little two-paragraph service features. If I reject the query, I might ask a writer to expand on a previously published article. Always include a self-addressed, stamped envelope.

The writer must know what *Penthouse* is. Read the magazine several times to see what we do and don't do. There's no point in suggesting literary essays or poetry or other things that we don't do. You'd be surprised at how many of those queries I get.

Writers must think far ahead. We have a very long lead time. A good rule of thumb is that it's going to be at least six months from the time the spark enters the writer's brain until the published article is in the hands of a reader. That weeds out a lot of inappropriate ideas and suggestions. The writer must ask himself or herself, "What is somebody going to want to read in six months? What information do I have that will be current then?"

We're very scrupulous in fact-checking. I always suggest that nonfiction writers send in an annotated version of the article showing where the facts came from. That kind of road map can save endless amounts of time and phone calls from editors if questions come up. As our society gets more litigious, this is helpful to the writer as well as the publisher. If the writer doesn't send it in, he or she should have that information very quickly available.

30

Writing for *Modern Bride* and Other Bridal Magazines

CELE LALLI, VICE PRESIDENT AND
EDITOR IN CHIEF
Modern Bride
New York

CELE LALLI holds a degree in early childhood education. After graduation from college, she headed for New York to teach school, but was bitten by the publishing bug and landed a job as a trainee in the science fiction department at Ziff-Davis. Her tasks included the reading of unsolicited manuscripts. Lalli soon developed the "goose flesh factor"— when she got goose flesh, the manuscript was a winner. In five years, Lalli climbed the ranks to editor. During that time, she discovered and developed friendships with writers who became famous in the field, among them Ben Bova, Roger Zelazny, Tom Disch, Ursula le Guin, Keith Laumer, and Harlan Ellison. She also worked with legendary writers, including Robert Heinlein, Isaac Asimov, and Ray Bradbury. In 1965 she switched gears at Ziff-Davis and joined *Modern Bride*. She was quickly promoted to executive editor and became editor in chief in 1982. She is now vice president and editor in chief.

Modern Bride was launched in 1949 by Ziff-Davis Publishing as the first newsstand bridal publication. The bimonthly circulation is 370,427. Most articles are freelance-written. "We only have one staff writer," says Lalli.

□ **How many queries do you receive?**
About twenty a week. Every once in a while we find a jewel.

□ **What chance does a first-time writer have of getting published in *Modern Bride*?**
A first-time writer has a very good chance if he or she is a good writer and the article is of immediate interest to the bride-to-be.

□ **What do you look for in submissions?**
We are receptive to freelance submissions on wedding planning, real weddings that the writer has seen or participated in, interpersonal relationships, sex and marriage, establishing mutual goals, and financial planning. (Queries on these topics should be directed to Managing Editor, Mary Ann Cavlin.) We do not want over-the-transom queries on travel articles because we have a stable of established travel writers who are familiar with our format and style.

□ **How quickly do you respond to queries?**
Within a month.

□ **What happens after a query sparks your interest?**
We write to express interest in the query. If the writer does not have credentials, we make it clear that the article must be submitted on spec. If the writer has professional credentials and we like his or her clips, we agree to consider the proposed article with a kill fee if it doesn't live up to expectations.

□ **What is a typical article that you might assign a freelance writer?**
There are several typical articles we might assign. One wedding piece might be focused on regional weddings, with interviews of the couple and wedding professionals. Another would be related to the interpersonal changes that occur during the transition from engagement to marriage. For example, issues related to dealing with in-laws and financial concerns are two possibilities.

□ **How does the editor-author relationship evolve?**
The editor tells the writer the points to be covered. We ask the writer to be familiar with the style of articles published in *Modern Bride* and to be succinct. We prefer articles to be about 1,500 words. Our outside limit is 2,000 words.

□ **What if you don't like the completed article?**
If it doesn't hit the mark, we ask the author to rewrite it. If the writer has done a thorough job in terms of research, organization, and content and the rewrite is still not adequate, we prefer to polish it up rather than continue with rewrites. If the piece is still not acceptable after the writer works hard to rewrite it, we issue a kill fee. We probably will not go back to that person for future assignments. If the writer is unwilling to make suggested changes, we will not pay a kill fee.

□ What do you look for in writers?

We want writers who are very professional, who deliver well-organized, thoroughly researched, fully informative, neatly written manuscripts. We keep in touch with writers who consistently deliver good work. We think about them when new challenges come along. We sometimes get inquiries from publishers who want to do wedding-related books. We refer them to writers we can count on. It is a mutually rewarding experience.

□ What are your pet peeves about writers?

Writers who don't do their homework, who don't read the magazine and aren't familiar with its style and content.

□ Do you have advice for writers?

Carefully research the marketplace and be certain the query or manuscript you submit is truly relevant to the magazine's niche.

If you really believe you've got something on target, keep the submissions flowing. The old adage "nothing ventured, nothing gained" is one worth following. Some of the most successful writers got plenty of rejection slips before their first piece was published. I have been responsive to writers because of that. It also helps cultivate patience, flexibility, and courtesy in your professional communications.

31

Writing for Romance/Confession Magazines

SUE WEINER, EDITORIAL DIRECTOR

Sterling-Macfadden Publishers
New York

SUE WEINER majored in English and education in college. After graduation, when she couldn't get a teaching job, she changed her career path.
After a short stint in children's book publishing, she landed a job in 1979
at Macfadden, publishers of the world's major romance magazines. (Macfadden merged with Sterling in 1993.) Weiner climbed the ranks from
assistant editor to associate editor, editor, and finally her present position
as editorial director of all of the Sterling-Macfadden magazines.

Sterling-Macfadden magazines include *True Story, True Confessions,
True Romance, True Love, Modern Romances,* and *True Experience.* Romance magazines are sold on newsstands and through subscriptions.

Founded in 1919 by Bernard Macfadden, *True Story* is Sterling-Macfadden's number one magazine, with a monthly circulation of over one
million. Unlike most romance publications, it publishes women's service
articles as well as romance stories. *True Story* readers are primarily women
eighteen to fifty and over. "People have been reading *True Story* from the
beginning and they still read it," says Weiner.

☐ Why are true confession magazines so popular?

Because people want to read about other people's lives that they can relate to.
We have a very strong readership. Our readers are very middle America. They're
high school–educated or have had some college training. We used to call our
readers "pink-collar" women (counterpart to blue-collar workers). They're not

the sophisticated women who might buy *Vogue*. Some women buy all the magazines and some are loyal to just one.

□ How have romance magazines evolved?

They've changed the same way our readers' lives have changed. More women are working. There's much more wife abuse now, a big issue in our magazine. It always has been, but after OJ, it's more prevalent. We offer advice to readers about where to go and what to do. Now, instead of alcoholism, there's more drugs. We always publish relationship and love stories. That doesn't change very much through the years. Women are always trying to find a good man to love them.

□ Describe the stories that are published in your magazines.

They're true stories about relationships and other things that can happen in a woman's life. In fact, writers must sign releases before we can publish them. We change the names and locations—we don't keep any real names in the stories. The stories are always told in the first person and written as people really speak. The language is conversational.

A sympathetic person, the narrator, tells her own story in her own voice. Something happened. She got in trouble. But she's not a bad woman. She could be your friend. You know, when your friend comes over and tells you what's going on in her life.

□ Is there always a moral to the story?

There doesn't have to be. But we wouldn't do a story about a hopeless murderer. Our readers want a story about somebody they could really know—a friend or neighbor—and what goes on behind closed doors.

□ Are the stories formulaic?

In a way. To learn the style of our magazines, I suggest people read a few copies.

□ Let's talk about "behind closed doors." Do the stories include blatant sex or sexual innuendo?

We're careful that they don't go too far sexually. We draw the curtain. Passionate or romantic, but no sex. The story may say "they made passionate love," but we're not going to describe it. The reader has to use her imagination. If a story is too sexy, we'll clean it up.

□ Give me some examples of successful stories you published and how your readers related to them.

We had a very sad story about a baby who died a crib death. We got many letters from people who experienced the same thing. It helped by showing them that they're not alone. We publish stories about husbands who cheat on their wives. These stories show readers that they're not the only person whose husband has cheated. We recently ran a piece about a woman whose father raped her, she had the baby, her mother raised the baby girl, and she never told her sister that she was the mother. We received an overwhelming number of letters from readers who had similar experiences, who never before told anyone.

☐ Who are your writers?

They are primarily our readers. Most are amateurs. All they need is a story to tell. They have to write from the heart. Some are fabulous writers. Others touch your heart because they've written purely and, if needed, we do some editorial work. Writers don't have to worry about grammar. We'll clean it up.

☐ Do professional romance writers submit stories to you?

A few. Some can write what we need as long as it is based on truth.

☐ How could I write in the first person if it didn't happen to me?

If it happened to someone you know, you can take on the voice. But it has to be true.

☐ Are you *the* market for short romance stories?

Yes. We own the market.

☐ How do you usually acquire your stories?

They come in the mail. We get so many manuscripts over the transom that we can usually find any story we want. Thirty or forty or more come to *True Story* alone each day. We read them all. We would never not read a manuscript. We always want manuscripts, not queries.

☐ How much do you pay writers?

We pay about three to five cents per word. The stories run about one thousand to ten thousand words. We offer a contract for each story and we buy all rights.

☐ Are romance magazines a good place for someone to break in who ultimately wants to write romance novels? How do your stories compare to romance books?

It's definitely a good place to break in. Our stories are more realistic than romance novels. There's not always a happy ending. The woman doesn't always get the man. There's not as much formula. Our stories focus on a lot of different issues, more than would be found in a romance book.

☐ Why would a professional writer contribute to your magazines?

It's a good place to get started if you want to get published. We can help you develop as a writer.

☐ Do you have advice for writers who have a true story to sell?

Don't be afraid. Take the chance and tell your story. Write it the way you would tell a friend. Tell it from the heart. It must touch the person who is reading it.

32

Writing for *AutoWeek* and Other Automobile Magazines

MATT DeLORENZO, EDITOR
AutoWeek
Detroit

MATT DeLORENZO was a journalism major in college. After graduation, he worked as a reporter for a daily newspaper. Cars have always
been DeLorenzo's hobby. He took a job as editor of *Automotive Fleet*, a
special-interest trade magazine that dealt primarily with the fleet and
leasing industry. In 1982 he went to *Automotive News*, a trade newspaper
for the automotive industry, where he combined his newspaper skills with
his knowledge of automobiles. In 1989 he became editor of *AutoWeek*, a
consumer automotive magazine.

AutoWeek started out in 1958 as a weekly newspaper that covered
automobile racing. In 1986 it was downsized to a magazine styled after
Time and *Newsweek*, targeted to automotive enthusiasts. *AutoWeek* covers new car launches, product information news, and racing. Its present
weekly circulation is almost 300,000. "We're a unique magazine in the
United States in that we cover both new cars—what we call 'sheet
metal'—and motor sports on a weekly basis," says DeLorenzo.

☐ **How much of *AutoWeek* is written by freelance writers?**
About a third.

☐ **How do you acquire articles that are not written in-house?**
We usually work with established freelance writers whom we hire on a retainer
basis. Domestically, most of our news and features are written in-house, but our

auto racing coverage is farmed out to regular freelancers who cover racing. One is a newspaper man from Pittsburgh, who covers Indy for us. That's all he does. Another is an established British motorsports journalist who travels all over the world and does all of our Formula I coverage. I have another writer on retainer in Italy who covers new cars there.

□ Are credentials important for your freelance writers?

Credentials mean something. If a writer has been published in a major magazine, my interest goes up.

□ How can beginning writers break in at *AutoWeek*?

It's difficult because we are an established name. A long time ago, when we were more of a fanzine (a term used to describe publications written by fans), people who just knew about cars could get published. Since we downsized into the magazine format, upgraded our staff, and produce a slicker package, we now act more like *Sports Illustrated* or *Time*. To a greater extent, we rely on our staff for major features.

Freelance writers must know our publication. I can't stress that enough. It's really difficult to break in at our magazine because we're special-interest and our readers are fans. I see so many unsolicited manuscripts from freelancers who have read the magazine and don't quite understand what it's about, or from regular readers, who know what we're about but are not writers. I'm looking for a writer who is knowledgeable about the subject and can write.

Everybody who reads our magazine is an enthusiast or likes cars. They often write and say, "What if you stuck me in a race car?" Well, I don't want to hear about you driving a race car. The readers don't want to hear that. They want to hear what it's like to drive in a race car from a professional.

We're the experts and we know how to write for our readers. Freelance writers have to be more like us in terms of being experts. They have to be able to get into a situation or have access to something that our readers can't get to and we can't get to. They must present it to us in an entertaining and interesting fashion. It's tough.

□ Give me an example of the way a writer can get your attention.

Ralph Lauren is a car buff. He has won Pebble Beach three or four times. If a writer knows something special or has an angle—"I was in on the acquisition or restoration of a car that Ralph Lauren found in East Germany and I can write this story in a compelling and convincing fashion"—I'll buy that story. But if I don't know the writer and he's just saying, "I sold an old car to Ralph Lauren," I won't buy it.

I'll listen to someone who says, "I've got this story that you can't resist." Your story must be very special, you must be able to write, and you have to have written somewhere else. My reaction has to be, "Wow! This is something I've *got* to have!"

We pay attention if a writer has a story that is irresistible—not something that grows out of your everyday fascination with cars. We're interested in a piece that we can't get.

We don't want a writer to tell us what it's like to go to an Indy car race. It's like saying, "I've been to the Super Bowl. I'll write a story for *Sports Illustrated* about the Super Bowl." *Sports Illustrated* won't buy that from an unknown writer. But they'll buy "George Plimpton goes to the Super Bowl." That's the mode we're in. Our readers expect certain things from us.

□ **Tell me about unsolicited manuscripts that are sent to you.**
I get about eight to ten unsolicited manuscripts a week. To be honest, I send practically all of them back.

□ **How much do you pay that rare freelancer who breaks in?**
It varies. Our top rate is a dollar per word.

□ **Tell me about your freelancers in terms of rights.**
Our rights work against freelancers. We own product stories, for which the writer drives a car and does driving impressions of a new vehicle. We prefer to have those staff-written because we sell those stories. We're syndicated in many newspapers and that's a substantial business for us.

□ **Do you have pet peeves about things that freelance writers do?**
Writers who call me on the phone. That's number one. That's really difficult when I'm working on a deadline. I don't mind a fax or letter query.

□ **What advice do you have for writers who want to be published in** *AutoWeek* **or comparable publications?**
Editors want writers with a track record. Very few people burst on the writing scene, especially when you're dealing with special-interest subjects. Write for lesser publications. Work your way up. Find a specialty and stick with it. Very few people are Leonardo DeVincis—masters of all. You can't write about airplanes tomorrow, motorcycles yesterday, and cars today.

Publishing is not a monastery. Editors talk to other editors. We know who's out there and who's good.

Writing for *PC Computing* and Other Computer Magazines

JON ZILBER, MANAGING EDITOR

Infoseek Guide
Former Editor in Chief
PC Computing
Foster City, California

JON ZILBER double-majored in math and physics in college and holds a master's degree in technology and policy. A mass media/engineering fellowship convinced Zilber that journalism would be more interesting than a career as a pure technologist. In 1986 he joined the staff of *MacUser* magazine as features editor and quickly rose to editor in chief. He then went to *PC Computing* as editor in chief in 1994. Zilber is now managing editor of *InfoSeek Guide*, an on-line publication and navigational tool. At the time of this interview John Zilber was editor in chief of *PC Computing*.

PC Computing was launched in 1987 and, according to Zilber, is one of the fastest growing publications in the United States, with a monthly circulation of one million.

☐ **Tell me about personal computer users and PC *Computing*'s target audience.**
The largest segment of personal computer users don't care about their computers. Someone in the office bought the PC, told them what software to use, and showed them which buttons to push. They neither need nor want more information.

A second group of PC users are at the opposite end of the spectrum. These people take the hood off the computer, tinker with it, tweak it, and squeeze every ounce of power out of it. They're always buying new stuff so they can get more out of the computer. They recognize a need for information and buy magazines.

Then there are people whose careers circle around the computer. They work for informations departments or their job description involves PCs.

Some users have no professional or formal responsibility for PCs, but have empowered themselves as the office PC guys, the computer gurus. Everyone goes to these people with questions.

The latter group is our target audience. They may have no PCs in their job description, but recognize that computers are powerful, competitive tools. If they don't exploit the latest PC technology, their competitors will. Most of our articles center around a computer product and comparisons of different products in a category. We're currently working on an article about tools for publishing electronically for live presentations—how to get a point across on paper, in person, and electronically. *PC Computing* features typically present a problem and the solutions available from the reader's PC.

□ **Tell me about articles that you usually entrust to freelance writers.**
Articles that we call "mind-food stories" are written by freelancers. The focus is not on products, but on something a little more abstract, something that is intrinsically more interesting. Mind-food stories are not going to come from our staff or from our traditional pool of freelancers who test products all day long. An example of a mind-food story that we published was called "Virus, They Wrote." The freelancer had access to the community of people who write computer viruses. He interviewed them as well as people who study this phenomenon. There are all kinds of conspiracy theories about where computer viruses come from. Some people think that they're created or sponsored by those who sell the software that cures computer viruses. Some people believe they're sponsored by terrorists. Others believe they're simply pranks.

Another mind-food story that we published was about the use of notebook computers by passengers on commercial airlines. At the time, some airlines were concerned that these computers might interfere with an airplane's navigational equipment. The article questioned whether it was a serious hazard when someone across the aisle used a notebook computer during takeoff and landing or whether the airlines were just trying to find a scapegoat for their own safety problems.

□ **How do you usually acquire articles?**
We usually assign them to our existing pool of freelancers. We try to keep our pool as small as possible and keep all of our freelancers as busy as possible. About twenty freelancer writers contribute to every issue, and about 50 percent of all of our articles are written by freelancers.

□ How can beginning freelance writers break in at *PC Computing*?

First and foremost, they must know the publication. We receive lots of queries that don't fit our magazine. If the idea doesn't fit, we don't look any further.

What we really want from freelancers are new ideas. We're usually sold on ideas, not on the writer's credentials. We operate on the premise that if you come up with a great idea for a story that fits our editorial target, you'll get the first shot at it, whether you have experience or not.

Another approach for beginning writers is to look at various sections of the magazine. For example, we do reviews of about twenty new products a month. There's no real idea here, but it's a good place for freelancers to break in. We're looking for expertise. The writer must explain what makes him or her qualified to review a particular product.

Be aware of industry trends. Several years ago the whole internet phenomenon took off. Most freelancers we've added recently have been internet-related. All of a sudden computer writers need to have internet expertise.

□ Do you want to see clips from first-time writers?

I usually make a decision on the basis of the query letter, not the clips. I don't put a whole lot of stock in them. If it's a published clip, I never know if the writer is good or if he or she had a good editor. Most people either send no clips or far too many. I want three pages max. I don't have much time to evaluate a new writer.

□ How much do you pay writers?

We pay first-time writers in the neighborhood of fifty cents per word. It's unusual for us to pay any writer more than a dollar per word.

□ What are your pet peeves?

Queries that don't fit this magazine. I receive queries time and again from people who may have a lot to offer, but didn't look at the magazine. They don't know the difference between this magazine and eight other competitors. An editor who receives that query will not pursue the writer, however interesting he or she may be.

Another pet peeve is writers who don't follow the specs. If we've outlined the story for eight hundred words, it should be eight hundred words. The writer who turns in a thousand-word story is saying, "I'm too lazy," or "That's the editor's job." The editors say, "We're paying you to write this and part of your job is getting it the right length."

I don't like receiving a dry treatise when we've asked for something fun. And vice versa.

□ Is it okay for authors to phone you with an idea?

It's a crapshoot. They'll always reach me, my assistant, or my voice mail. The idea will eventually get to me. If it sounds good, the writer will hear back. It's usually easiest to reach editors at computer magazines by E-mail. Most computer magazines list their E-mail addresses somewhere in the magazine.

□ Do you answer all E-mail and phone queries?

I answer most E-mail. Everybody in the computer press is bombarded by junk mail, whether it comes in the mailbox, by E-mail, or over the phone. It's physically impossible to answer everything.

□ Do you have advice or words of warning for freelancers who want to be published in *PC Computing* and comparable computer magazines?

Know the publication that you want to write for. Read it and understand its tone. Pay attention to the specs. An author who turns in camera-ready copy is usually assured of getting more work.

Computer press editors are in the business of filtering out information. We spend most of our time deciding what *not* to publish. Whatever's left is what we end up doing. We're looking for reasons to rule out people.

34

Writing for *Fortune* and Other Business and Finance Magazines

WALTER KIECHEL, FORMER MANAGING EDITOR
Fortune
New York

WALTER KIECHEL majored in English literature and history in college. After graduation, he served for five years in the navy, earned a law degree and a master's degree in business administration, passed the bar examination, and decided not to pursue a career in law. In 1977 he joined *Fortune* magazine as a reporter/researcher. Kiechel became the managing editor in May 1994 and served in that capacity until February 1995. At the time of this interview, Walter Kiechel was managing editor of *Fortune*.

Fortune was founded in February 1930 by Henry Luce. According to Kiechel, *Fortune* seeks to be the world's most respected and influential source of ideas, explanations, and solutions for decision makers and smart people in business. The magazine's biweekly circulation is about 870,000.

☐ **Which magazines are *Fortune's* closest competitors?**
BusinessWeek and *Forbes* are our closest competitors. *BusinessWeek* is a news weekly of business while *Forbes* appeals to readers who are interested in investing. In some sense we also compete against the *Harvard Business Review* and the *Wall Street Journal*. We, at *Fortune*, are in the business of purveying ideas for people who are in decision-making, executive, and managerial jobs. In that respect, we're different from our competitors. One of the trends that I've seen in the past ten years is an evolving ecology of the business magazine world. The roles for the different publications have become more distinct.

☐ Who reads *Fortune*?

Fortune is read by people who are engaged in some sort of business activity. Forty percent of our readers hold an executive title, like vice president or above. Twenty-five percent work for organizations that employ twenty-five people or less. Another 25 percent work at organizations that employ ten thousand people or more. The median age is in the early forties. *Fortune* readers are typically affluent people in business or with businesses of their own. Psychographically, they are very competitive people. (Psychographics are psychological leanings— what these people worry about.)

We have many readers in the executive suites, including chief executive officers, but we're not written exclusively for top executives. We're written for smart people who need ideas, who are interested in the changes going on around them, and who are looking for opportunities to prosper.

Our readers want our take on the future, forward-looking trends, and what that means for them now. They also want ideas and explanations of what's going on around them. I believe that we're in the course of a major economic transition comparable to the transition from the agricultural to a manufacturing economy. We call this new world the new economy. Other people call it the information economy. It is a fundamental, secular change. People are very interested. They ask, "Can you make sense of this for me?" and "What do I need to know in order to thrive and prosper in this new world?"

☐ What are typical examples of *Fortune* articles?

Two-thirds of *Fortune*'s editorial pages are devoted to what we call the middle of the book, where you would find seven to ten stories. Of those, two or three are in a category that we call managing. Managing could be stories on how to manage better, improve distribution systems, increase the power of purchasing managers, or empower maverick managers, or stories that profile extremely well-managed companies. There would also be stories about the economy such as "How to prepare for the next recession" or "Looking at housing prices—houses as an investment in the United States and abroad." You might find a story about personal investing. We did a cover story on the coming investor revolt—how investors are increasingly unhappy with the fees that they're charged. They want the money managers' compensation linked to the performance of their funds. We publish stories on information technology that could be a thirteen-page profile of Bill Gates and Microsoft or a four-page story on Lotus Notes. We also run stories on trends. I did a cover story about how we'll work in the year 2000. In our Executive Life category, you might find a story on depression as it relates to businesspeople or how people can plan their next career. Of course, there will be some global coverage. That might be on Nestlé and how it runs its package goods business in Asia, Latin America, and Europe or a story on the spread of malls throughout the world.

□ What percentage of your articles are freelance-written?
Very few. Less than 5 percent. We do have a stable of two or three freelance writers.

□ Do you receive a lot of unsolicited queries and manuscripts?
Yes. I can't say that they're all read. We are hesitant to encourage writers to send complete manuscripts because the volume is so high.

□ What would spark your interest in a query or manuscript that came in over the transom?
It would reflect an understanding of our editorial mission, what we are about as a magazine, and how we are distinct from our competitors. The writer could glean this from an attentive reading of the magazine. Most important, the writer would offer an idea or a concept or a way of understanding things that we hadn't seen before and that we think would be relevant to our readers.

□ What exactly are you looking for in a freelance writer and the writer's clips?
We're looking for writers who have written somewhere else. They have to have a track record. The clips must demonstrate an ability to write our kinds of articles in some other form. I look for rudimentary writing skills, analytical ability, ability to marshal arguments, and the ability to put things together in a fresh way.

We're different from other publications in that our articles run six to eight pages. We're bucking the trend toward smaller pieces, one-pagers or four-paragraph deals. Our articles entail gathering a lot of information, ordering it very well, and bringing out insights clearly. The writer must be very skilled.

□ How much do you pay freelance writers, and do you offer contracts?
From $3,000 to $8,000. We offer contracts on an article-by-article basis.

□ Do you have advice for freelancers to want to write for *Fortune* or comparable magazines?
Know the publication. Know our general mission and what we're about. Don't pitch a story of massively local interest that we're never going to run. Don't query us on an idea that is completely unlike anything you've seen in our pages.

Writers should have some specialization or be in a field in which they are particularly expert. At the same time they must have good generalist skills—to write and think and make arguments and reason critically. It's a tension between the two.

I don't want to discourage writers, but it's very hard. There's that catch-22. Most writers who come to our attention are the ones who have already gotten a certain amount of attention.

There are more people who wish to write for publication than there are places to write for. However, I think there are more opportunities now for people to publish than there have ever been, whether on-line or for smaller publications. That should be encouraging to potential writers.

35

Writing for *Harper's* and Comparable General-Interest Magazines

LEWIS LAPHAM, EDITOR

Harper's
New York

LEWIS LAPHAM majored in English literature at Yale college. After graduation in 1956, he attended Cambridge University in England with the thought of becoming a historian. He subsequently went to work as a newspaper reporter, first for the *San Francisco Examiner* and then for the *New York Herald Tribune*. During the 1960s, Lapham was a contributing editor to *The Saturday Evening Post*, *Life*, and *Harper's Magazine*. In March 1971 he became an editor "by accident" as the result of a sudden shuffling of management at *Harper's*. "On Monday I was a writer," he said, "and on Tuesday I was an editor." He served as managing editor of *Harper's Magazine* until 1975, when he was promoted to editor in chief. Another shuffling of management at *Harper's Magazine* in 1981 prompted Lapham to resign, but he returned in 1984 as editor, the position he still holds. "Think of me," he said once, "as the Grover Cleveland of the American magazine business."

Founded in 1850, *Harper's Magazine* is the oldest continuously published magazine in the United States, with a current monthly circulation of 220,000. It is a magazine of general interest, dealing with political and literary subjects and addressed to an audience of intelligent readers. Lapham defines intelligent readers as people who like to read, know the difference between good and bad writing, take an interest in ideas, and welcome the possibilities implicit in the American experiment.

□ **Which publications compete with *Harper's*?**
The New Republic, *The Atlantic*, *The New Yorker*, *The New York Review of Books*, *American Heritage*, *Foreign Affairs*, *American Spectator*, *Policy Review*, and the literary quarterlies, particularly *Grand Street*, *Hudson Review*, *Paris Review*, and *Georgia Review*.

□ **What makes *Harper's* unique from a writer's point of view?**
Harper's looks for a distinctive tone of voice. If a writer comes to *Harper's Magazine* and asks, "What kind of an article do you want?" I ask, "What kind of an article do *you* want? What do you want to write? What do you know about? What do you care about?" *Harper's* welcomes the writer's thought and experience and prefers narratives told in the first-person singular. I'm not much interested in policy papers, abstract theory, or political analysis.

□ **Give me a mix of articles in a typical *Harper's* issue.**
A typical issue includes a long reporting piece (9,000 to 10,000 words), an essay, a memoir, a short story, an annotation, and a book review.

□ **Can a first-time writer be published in *Harper's* if he or she does a good job with that query?**
A good query has a chance, and so does an unsolicited manuscript. Our interns read everything in the slush pile. They bring to an editor's attention anything they think is deserving of a second reading.

□ **What sparks your interest in a query?**
It may be the name of the writer whose work I will know, or it may be the subject. But it will always be the tone of voice. If I can hear in the query the voice of a writer with something to say, I will be interested.

The query letter should be a proposal, not just, "Hi! Would you like a piece on X?" I'd throw those out. It has to be, "I've noticed such and such. I know about X and Y. I'd like to write from this point of view at this kind of length."

The query should be two pages of typescript—long enough for me to get a sense of who the writer is. From an unknown writer, a one-page query is too short.

□ **Are credentials and clips important to being published in *Harper's*?**
Credentials help. What's more important is whether the person can write. If the query letter is good, I don't bother with the clips.

In a year, probably three or four of our pieces are written by first-time writers. The percentage is about 5 percent.

□ Do you have a cadre of writers to whom you assign work?

Yes. Seventy percent of our pieces are assigned. We have a list of maybe two hundred people whose work we admire. We would be delighted if any one of those writers would contribute something to the magazine. Once a beginning writer gets published at *Harper's*, he or she becomes part of that cadre.

□ Will an article published in *Harper's* open doors for beginning writers?

Yes. *Harper's* over the past five years has published fifteen or twenty first pieces from beginning writers. These writers had never been previously published anywhere else. Every one of them now has a book contract.

□ Tell me about your pay scale.

Our pay scale ranges from $2,000 to $5,000, depending on the writer and the length of the manuscript.

□ Do you have any pet peeves about writers?

Writers who send in manuscripts so poorly typed that they're difficult to read.

□ What should writers do if they want to be published in *Harper's* or comparable magazines?

They should read the magazines. They should be familiar with a magazine's editorial stance or point of view. *Harper's* almost never takes a piece likely to appear in *The Atlantic*. *Harper's* and *The Atlantic* have a very different feeling and tone.

If a writer has read *Harper's* and understands the sensibility of the magazine, his or her understanding will show up in the query letter—both in the way the letter is written and in the subject about which the writer proposes to write.

36

Writing for *Parade*

LARRY SMITH, MANAGING EDITOR
Parade
New York

LARRY SMITH, after graduating from college with a degree in English, worked for seventeen years as a reporter at six different newspapers, including the *New York Times* and the *New York Daily News*. His novel, *The Original*, was published in 1972 by Herder & Herder and Bantam Books. Over the course of those years he also did some freelance writing. He has had short fiction published in *Redbook* and has written for *The Daily News Sunday Magazine* and the *New York Times* travel section. Smith has been managing editor of *Parade* since 1982.

Founded in the early 1940s, *Parade* appeared on the newsstands for just a few weeks when it metamorphosed into a magazine supplement for Sunday newspapers. *Parade's* present circulation is 37.1 million, which, according to Smith, translates into 81 million readers. *The Guinness Book of Records* notes that *Parade* has the largest circulation in the world.

□ **How do you categorize *Parade*, and what is its vision?**
Parade is a general-interest magazine with a very distinctive point of view. Its intent is to inform and entertain, but informing to us means enlightening and encouraging readers to recognize that while there are a great many things in the world that need fixing, there's no need to look on in despair and say that nothing can be done.

The fundamental idea is that human beings transform themselves. All of us grow each day. We believe that people can make a better world. *Parade* appeals to the noble motives of readers, without corn or cliché.

□ What makes *Parade* stand out from other publications?

Our huge audience, for one. Because of our readers, almost everyone wants to write for us. I mean *everybody*. Folks who won't talk to other publications are eager to be interviewed for *Parade*.

Most important, we don't stereotype. We don't categorize. We don't have formulas. We try to stay as fresh, as original, as lively as the day itself. *Parade* is a model of expository English. Not surprisingly, *Parade* is used in classrooms across the country. We get requests continuously to reprint articles for use in textbooks and classrooms.

We respect our readers. They are like us. We edit to be read. We do have a vast readership, but we're read one copy at a time. College professors and physicists take issue with *Parade* columnist Marilyn vos Savant, and teenagers write to the "Fresh Voices" column.

□ Give me some examples of typical *Parade* articles.

In the fall of 1994 we published an exploration of emotional abuse. The subject needed reporting. The *Parade* piece dramatically and clearly defined a problem that shapes all our lives. Almost everyone is subjected to emotional abuse from the moment he or she can listen. Those who emotionally abuse us often think of themselves as well meaning.

Other provocative ideas have included a single mother writing on why she bought a gun, and borrowing money from relatives.

□ What is the average length of your feature articles?

Fifteen hundred words.

□ Do you think up article ideas, or do you wait for them to come to you?

Both. We're democratic. Anyone can suggest a story. Ideas may come from individuals, agents—anyone. We receive tens of thousands of unsolicited queries a year. Very few are published.

□ Do your writers need credentials?

It's easier if people know who you are but we also publish a lot of first-time writers.

□ What sparks your interest in a query?

A brilliant idea. An idea that's almost in front of your face, like the emotional abuse one that I was talking about. The query letter should be three paragraphs, max. The writer should be familiar with the subject and put what's most significant in those paragraphs.

□ **How long does it take you to get back to the writer?**
It varies. A week, a couple weeks, sometimes longer. We receive *thousands* of queries.

□ **How do you feel about phone calls from writers?**
With thousands of queries, it's pretty close to impossible to discuss stories over the telephone. We prefer queries in writing.

□ **Do you offer contracts and kill fees, and how much money do you pay authors?**
We offer contracts and kill fees. Nobody gets paid less than $1,000.

□ **What endears certain writers to you?**
Skill. Making deadlines. Responding to revises. We often ask writers to rewrite articles two or three times.

□ **Do you have pet peeves?**
I hate bad writing. I hate sloppy ideas. I hate laziness and carelessness. I don't like dilettantes. I don't like writers who are sloppy in their thinking or who use everyday clichés like "spearhead" or "kickoff" and misuse "déjà vu" and say "most importantly" and all of those other egregiously atrocious things found in public print day in and day out.

□ **What is the biggest mistake that aspiring writers make?**
Writers often think if they sit down and start writing, it will come. That's not true. You can't just write off the top of your head. You must do your research, homework.

□ **What is the most important advice you could give freelancers who want to write for *Parade* and comparable publications?**
The idea is everything. Writers peddle the same stories over and over, like profiles of Frank Sinatra. We need unique ideas. Think big. If you're trying to measure your idea against something, try to conceive of it as something you might see on "60 Minutes" (the television program). Remember, our audience is larger than that of "60 Minutes." Read the magazine you hope to write for. Sound simple? Many do not.

If you want to do something easy, be a brain surgeon. If you want to do something difficult, be a freelance writer.

37

Writing for *Good Housekeeping* and Other Top Women's Service Magazines

JOAN THURSH, FORMER ARTICLES EDITOR
Good Housekeeping
New York

JOAN THURSH was an English major in college. After graduation, she worked for a variety of publishing houses. She ultimately landed a job at *Good Housekeeping* as an associate editor in the articles department and climbed the ranks to articles editor.

Good Housekeeping, founded more than one hundred years ago, is a consumer magazine for women. Its monthly circulation is over 5 million. *Good Housekeeping*'s closest competitors are the other six "Seven Sisters" magazines, including *Ladies' Home Journal*, *McCall's*, *Women's Day*, *Family Circle*, *Redbook*, and *Better Homes & Gardens*.

□ **What are the most common *Good Housekeeping* articles?**
They fall into various categories, but the most successful are often personal narratives, dramatic personal stories in which the protagonist is almost always a woman.

□ **Who writes for *Good Housekeeping*?**
The majority of *Good Housekeeping* articles are by writers with whom we have successfully worked in the past. They may also write for other publications. If you look through various magazines, you often see the same bylines recurring. Nearly all of *Good Housekeeping*'s articles are freelance-written.

□ **How many unsolicited queries does *Good Housekeeping* receive?**
Good Housekeeping receives hundreds of queries each week. Every query is opened and read.

□ **What constitutes a good, professional query?**
The query should be no longer than it has to be to sell the proposed article. The author should tell just enough to pique our interest. The topic or story must be worth pursuing. The query should include gist or point of view of the article and reflect the writer's skills. If a writer can't organize and present the query in a coherent and selling manner, how can he or she do the article?

□ **When do you insist on seeing the article before making a commitment to buy it?**
When we have not worked with the writer before. When major magazines are not represented in the writer's clips that he or she has sent us (and presumably he or she has sent us the best clips). When we have doubts as to a whether a writer can handle the article. If it works out, we will negotiate with him or her upon acceptance of the manuscript and offer a contract for the article.

□ **Once a writer is published in *Good Housekeeping*, is he or she guaranteed more work?**
It doesn't guarantee assignments. But if we were pleased with the assignment, it does guarantee a more careful look at that author's next idea.

□ **What is your pay scale?**
It varies. It is almost never less than one dollar per word. The pay can be considerably more for a writer with whom we regularly work and who has come in with a big story for us.

□ **Do you give kill fees?**
Yes. We give 25 percent kill fees on assigned articles.

□ **Do you have pet peeves about writers?**
Phone calls. No editor likes to be bugged on the phone. It's a waste of time when a writer calls to say, "I have a hot scoop for you," and it turns out to be nothing.

□ **What do you advise writers who want to be published in *Good Housekeeping*?**
Get a handle on the kind of articles we publish. Writers often submit material on inappropriate subjects on the theory that since we haven't published anything on the topic, we must be looking for it. That's not the way it works. What we need is more of and/or better types of pieces that are successful for us.

Keep at it. There can be a lot of rejections. That's very difficult for writers. There's no easy way. On the other hand, an author can send in a terrific story and we will respond immediately. You just don't know. If you're lucky, you may come up with a really wonderful narrative for us or a scoop of some kind. Medical scoops are few and far between, but sometimes there is a twist or a take on medical information that has not been overdone by every other magazine in the country.

□ **If a writer has talent and perseveres, can he or she be published in** *Good Housekeeping* **and comparable magazines?**
Yes. But it takes a lot of perseverance. Rejections can be very discouraging. It's very tough because there are a lot of people submitting to us. And there are not that many wonderful stories out there.

38

Writing for *Redbook* and Comparable Women's Magazines

KATE WHITE, EDITOR IN CHIEF
Redbook
New York

KATE WHITE's college major was English. She began her publishing career as a feature writer for *Glamour*. White climbed the publishing ladder to become executive editor at *Family Weekly Weekend* and *Mademoiselle*. She has been editor in chief of *Child*, *Working Woman*, and *McCall's*. White joined *Redbook* as editor in chief in October 1994.

Founded in 1903 and acquired by Hearst Publications in 1982, *Redbook* is targeted to married women, ages twenty-five to forty-four. Articles deal primarily with relationships, fashion, and beauty. According to White, the magazine's mission is to be compelling and entertaining. *Redbook*'s monthly circulation is 3.2 million.

☐ **Give me the mix of articles found in a typical issue of Redbook.**
We publish two pieces with a news edge, two pieces that deal with women's lives today, at least one article about sexuality, and one or two articles about the workings of a marriage. There's usually a trend story, one or two parenting articles, a health story, something about personal psychology, and some pieces that are purely quirky and fun.

☐ **What types of ideas do you look for?**
We look for ideas that hit a nerve, issues that readers can relate to. Our editors come up with most ideas. At least 75 percent of our magazine's ideas are generated here.

□ What percentage of *Redbook* is freelance-written?

Ninety-eight percent. We use the top writers, particularly those with unique, interesting voices. Our writers must be able to tell a compelling, witty, or titillating story. Our writers are essayists, reporters, or fiction writers.

□ How does that differ from other magazines?

Magazines that go for pure information can live with a writer who is not much of a stylist, as long as he or she can do research.

□ Is it difficult for writers to break in at *Redbook*?

Yes. This is not the best magazine for beginning writers to break in at. The percentage of articles by beginning writers that work out is very low. Editors often have to do massive rewrites on these pieces so we almost always go with experienced, name writers.

Anyone interested in writing for us must first read and know the magazine. They should have winning ideas with strong working titles and fleshed-out proposals. And they should have clips that show that they can put a sentence together. If the writer has enough good clips, the editor may say, "Gee, this writer has really learned how to do this kind of piece; she has a lot of experience. I'm going to take a chance with her." Beginning writers should not start with *Redbook* or major magazines. They should start with smaller publications. Most top writers wrote for smaller publications and worked their way up.

Some writers who approach us actually have no concept of the magazine. The worst mistake these writers make is not reading the magazine. That has always struck me as ludicrous. A woman recently approached me at a social event and said, "I just sent you a long letter pitching a book review column." That violates the biggest rule in sales, which is, "Solve the other person's need, don't think of your own." The book review column was her agenda. All that woman had to do was look at *Redbook* to know that we don't cover the arts.

□ If a writer reads your magazine, figures out the style, comes up with a terrific idea, and sends you a couple very good clips, will that writer be published?

We would seriously look at the query. Whether it would have a real chance depends on the writer's expertise. If this was a service magazine and a writer submitted a fresh idea, I might say, "I know she may not do a super job, but we can work with this." If a service article is weak, it can be fixed in-house. But we run lots of essays and stylistic articles at *RB*, and the editor can't make up a writer's thoughts or style. What I'm trying to say is, we're open to someone who is experienced.

□ Do you have pet peeves about writers?

The biggest pet peeve is writers who submit inappropriate ideas because they're not familiar with the magazine.

Another is when sophisticated writers hand in an assignment that just didn't pan out rather than alert us as they were going along. Instead of calling and saying, "It sounded like a great idea, but I started looking into it and nothing's happening," they keep their fingers crossed and hope the editor won't notice.

□ Do you have advice for writers who want to break in at major magazines like *Redbook*?

Start small. Once you have accumulated clips, offer an editor a great idea. That editor may give you a shot at it.

Come up with a great working title for your proposed article. You can make an impression with a good title. That's how editors pitch ideas.

Some major magazines have sections with short articles that are a good place for writers to break in at. *Redbook* does not have those starter sections.

Would-be writers should work at a publication. It's a great way to see how magazines work, even if it's only for a year. You get the lay of the land. You get the dialect. You make contacts. If you know just one person at that magazine, he or she could eventually go to another publication and use you there. Most successful writers have had a stint working at a magazine.

The cream rises to the top. Publishing isn't like show business, where fabulous actors or singers don't get a break. There are clear paths for writers. But writers must follow a path and not set themselves up for discouragement.

39

Writing for *Reader's Digest*

PHILIP OSBORNE, ASSISTANT MANAGING EDITOR
Reader's Digest
Pleasantville, New York

PHILIP OSBORNE was an English and history major in college, graduating from night school. Along the way, he worked for several newspapers and a trade magazine before joining the Cleveland bureau of *Business Week*. He was brought into *Business Week*'s main New York office as a writer before moving to *Time* magazine as a contributing editor. After a writing stint at CBS, Osborne joined *Reader's Digest* in 1977, where he climbed the ranks from senior editor to assistant managing editor.

Reader's Digest was founded in February 1922 as a reprint magazine. It contained no original stories. The "originals program" was started in the 1950s when, according to Osborne, the *Digest* was having a difficult time finding enough strong material to fill the magazine. *Reader's Digest* now publishes approximately half original and half reprinted articles. It is sold on the newsstand and through subscription. Its monthly U.S. circulation is about 15 million, but *Reader's Digest* has 50 million readers in this country and 100 million readers around the world.

☐ **How is *Reader's Digest* unique?**
Reader's Digest is a mass, general-interest magazine—yet, in its way, it's as tightly focused and targeted as a special-interest magazine. Our goal is to educate, inform, inspire, and entertain. We want stories that touch the hearts and lives and minds of every one of our readers.

We're involved with our readers to an extent that no other magazine is. We get almost a half-million contributions a year. Readers send us articles from their local newspapers that move them. Or they write about personal experiences that might work as articles, short fillers, or department items.

□ Who is your audience?

It's everyone. We have readers in every age category. Our magazine probably has more eighteen- to thirty-five-year-old readers than the women's magazines that target this age group. In the same way, I'm sure we have more teenage readers than all the other magazines aimed at that age group.

□ Many freelance writers are daunted by *Reader's Digest* with its huge circulation. Can new writers break in?

Reader's Digest is the biggest magazine in the world. Writers are sometimes intimidated by numbers like that. They shouldn't be. I read every piece of writer mail that comes to me. I'm now working with a new writer who sent a query over the transom and eventually got an assignment. We publish many writers who have never even appeared in major national magazines.

Although we publish top writers, we also go after new writers. The magazine is constantly moving on to new subjects and new writers. We're always looking for new voices, new talent. That's the only way a magazine stays vital.

You don't have to have been published all over creation. You just need to have a good story to tell. There are so many touching personal stories out there that happen in the lives of individual people. You don't have to be a big-name writer to write such stories. You just have to be smart enough to recognize a story and smart enough to come to the *Digest* with it.

□ What are your article interests and needs?

We have covered everything in every direction since February 1922. We don't want to repeat ourselves. Every month we try to push the envelope, push into new areas. We're looking for new ideas and are determined to stay on the leading edge of what's going on in our world. That's the big challenge—finding what's new.

One category that turns me on is what we call the "promotable"—articles that appear on our newsstand band. They are usually service articles—ways people can improve themselves. For example, "How Not to Choke under Pressure" or "The Health Risk [osteoporosis] Women Can No Longer Ignore."

□ What do you want in a query letter or manuscript from a new writer?

Be short and to the point. And remember: You not only have to sell the idea. You have to sell yourself as the writer to execute that idea—to write that story. We discourage over-the-transom manuscripts from beginning writers. I usually don't read much farther than the first or second paragraph.

□ **What happens once you like an idea that comes in over the transom?**
We have an incredible bookkeeping process—a computerized listing system. If an idea comes in that I like and nobody has reserved it, I will enter it for the writer. The idea is then protected for that writer for six months. However, an idea that's in the news—a dramatic adventure story, for example—cannot be reserved. In that case, we simply go with the best writer.

Next, I check our index to make sure that we haven't done this topic before. Remember, publishing thirty articles a month means that we have done almost every legitimate topic in almost every conceivable way. But there's always a new twist, a new spin. That's what we're looking for.

After that, I look at what has been recommended by our reading staff, which covers 250 magazines and newspapers each month cover to cover. We also review two thousand books a year.

If, after I've checked the interest listings, I find that no one else has reserved the idea, and after I've checked the index, I find that we haven't done it, and after I've checked the articles recommended for reprint, I find that the idea hasn't been recommended, I may be interested. In that case, I'll ask the writer for a proposal.

□ **Does a proposal from a new writer have a chance against one from a top writer or someone on your staff?**
We want to see an article idea fully rounded out. This process is as much a protection for the writer as it is for the magazine. We want to be sure that the writer has a strong story. On the whole, we take ideas from new writers just as seriously as those from top writers. A proposal from a brand-new writer will rate equally against those of our regular staff people, except where our staff people have specialized knowledge and special contacts. We are looking for good stories. We don't care where they come from or whom they come from—as long as the writer is someone we feel we can count on.

□ **What do you want in a proposal?**
Proposals can run as long as three or four pages, single spaced. They are outlines. We don't want writers to write the whole piece, but we want to get a solid sense of how they're going to tell the story. First and foremost, we're storytellers at the *Digest*. Even major issue stories are often told as narratives. We want to see how the writer handles his or her material. It's like telling a joke. You can't describe a joke, you have to tell it. If I like the proposal, I might ask the writer to revise it. If a revision is not needed, all the better. I will send the proposal to our editor in chief, who reviews four to five each week. It's usually a quick process. If I submit a proposal by one of my writers on Thursday, I'll know by the following Tuesday if the writer has an assignment or not. A contract is then mailed to the writer.

Basically, we buy exclusive worldwide periodical rights. The contract spells out the length, rate, and everything else. We pay all legitimate expenses—travel, whatever. Of course, all expenses have to be documented. The writer gets the contract, signs it, and sends it back.

□ **Let's talk about article length.**
We buy in the long form (3,000–3,500 words). At most magazines, editing is done in succession—editors edit each other along the way. At the *Digest*, the editing or condensing is a layered process. Every editor along the way goes back to look at the writer's original wording. We try to faithfully preserve the writer's voice. There's one rule for our condensing process: "If it is not necessary to change, it is necessary *not* to change." In other words, don't change something just to change it. I've seen, at some magazines, editors edit the writer right out of the story. At *Reader's Digest*, the whole emphasis in condensing is to preserve the writer's distinctive voice.

Once a manuscript comes in, it may go back to the writer once or twice for repairs and fill-ins. Next, our editor in chief takes another look. If it's okay, it's purchased.

Once the article is purchased, it is sent to each of our five issue editors, in rotation. And it finds its way into the first available issue.

□ **Does *Reader's Digest* put writers through much rewrite or revision?**
Our standards are very demanding. There will often be revisions and rewrites. I have gone through three or four drafts with some new writers. When I first came to the *Digest*, I was working with one of our regular staff writers who summed it all up very well. She was a total professional, and she said to me, "I've been writing long enough for your magazine to know that you don't *write* for the *Digest*, you *rewrite* for the *Digest*." The important thing is that it's not only the magazine that benefits from this. So does the writer. He or she is much stronger for the experience.

□ **How much do you pay freelancer writers?**
Our bottom rate is $3,000, but that is for the simpler, easier article. If an article involves special research and leg-work, we'll nudge that starting rate up a few hundred dollars. We pay $3,500 for "Drama in Real Life." We also have a series called "Unforgettable Character," for which we pay $3,500. As a writer does more for the magazine, the rate goes up. Our rates are quite competitive.

□ **Do you have any special advice for writers?**
Bullet-proof your manuscript. When a story is scheduled, our fact-checking department begins its work. Our fact-checkers are second to none. We don't use secondary sources. You can't quote from newspapers or magazines. You've got to

go back to the primary sources to confirm that they weren't misquoted. If there's a faultline in a story, our fact-checking and research department will find it. A story can fall apart if the writer hasn't done his or her homework.

□ What's the key to breaking in at *Reader's Digest*?

Every writer asks that question. I tell them, "Please study our magazine." Writers always want the magic key. They want me to tell them, specifically, that I want this kind of article want that kind of story. We cover the broadest spectrum of topics, but we bring a distinctive approach and handling to everything we do. And you can learn that only by the most thorough studying of the magazine.

What are we looking for? We're looking for everything—we're looking for that perfect story. And for that perfect writer to tell it.

40

Writing for *Spy*

OWEN LIPSTEIN, EDITORIAL DIRECTOR AND
EDITOR IN CHIEF
Spy, Psychology Today, and Mother Earth News
New York

OWEN LIPSTEIN holds master's degrees in English literature from the University of Sussex in England and an MBA from Columbia University. His career began on the business side in magazine acquisitions at CBS and as circulation director for several special interest magazines. Lipstein's first publishing job was general manager for *Science '79, '80,* and *'81.* In 1981 Lipstein launched *American Health,* a "Cinderella success" that won a national magazine award for general excellence in 1985 and *Adweek*'s "Hottest Magazine in the Country" in 1986. Lipstein also invested in *Psychology Today* and several other magazines that "went bust." Lipstein became editorial director and editor in chief of *Psychology Today* (revived in 1991), *Mother Earth News,* and *Spy.*

Spy was founded in 1986 as a New York monthly magazine. It became a cultural phenomenon. *Spy*'s present circulation is 165,000.

☐ **Why is *Spy* so successful?**
Spy is a humor magazine. It's also a state of mind. Although the chronological age of our readers ranges widely (from twenty-five to forty-five), their state of mind is essentially adolescent—by that I mean they have no investment psychically in the status quo. In effect, for the *Spy* reader, nothing is sacred. The reader's state of mind essentially constitutes a rebellion against important political and cultural authority figures. It presupposes that what we are told by the conventional media is not true. That doesn't mean that all other media pull

punches. Only that there is a unique place in America and always has been that's willing to make fun of everyone and everything. It uses parody, satire, tough investigative reports, pranks, and cartoons as techniques. *Spy* magazine has not invented the genre of humor magazines. For years, it was the *National Lampoon* and before that it was *Harvard Lampoon* and at times *Esquire*. Now it is *Spy*. *Spy* is successful because a lot of people don't believe what they're being told and like to laugh at the self-inflated pomposities of cultural, political, and intellectual figures. We're fearless. And, like our readers, we have no investment in the status quo. We make fun of everybody. We're equally comfortable being bawdy and low-brow, high-faluting and ponderous.

□ **What publications does *Spy* compete with?**
There's no other national humor magazine but we compete with *Men's Journal*, *Rolling Stone*, *Esquire*, *New York*, and *GQ*. We compete for material and for readers.

□ **How do you usually acquire ideas or articles?**
We read the paper, listen to the radio, go to parties, get ideas from friends.

□ **Give me examples of typical *Spy* articles.**
I'm looking at an issue that has a picture of Sharon Stone reclining on a bed in a *Playboy* outfit. The article is titled "The New Power Bimbos—A *Spy* Exposé of Top Actresses Who Trade Nudity for Respectability." In this piece, we ranked the so-called big female movie stars in what we called the bimbo conspiracy. The lead goes, "Remember when actresses really could act? Remember all of the fun talk in the 1970s about feminine equality? Neither do we. Apparently, when it comes to landing choice roles, talent and ability has taken a back seat to breast implant nude scenes and *Playboy* spreads. Who are these women? Can they be stopped?" We looked at nude power bimbos, stealth bimbos, retro bimbos, nonbimbos, porno bimbos, nonbimbos who could be mistaken for bimbos, unintentional bimbos, the street factor, and the *Playboy* factor.

We did a question-and-answer piece story about the NRA (National Rifle Association). We called the head of the NRA and asked some stupid questions about guns that he actually answered. Like, "What is your favorite gun movie?"

We did a serious piece, but quite funny, on new weapons and what the generals have done with all of their money. They are creating kinder, gentler weapons—bowel-erupting sound machines and eyeball-bursting, organ-cloning lasers. There's actually a bomb that can be made from people poop—that's a way to upset the enemy.

□ **Tell me about *Spy* writers.**
As an example, we found our two senior writers by accident. They just graduated from Stanford and claimed to be seasoned pranksters. I was convinced when

they called Sylvester Stallone, identifying themselves as founders of *Q-Ball Magazine*, the magazine for bald people. Of course, Stallone's PR people said he's not bald. These kids persisted. "We have pictures. We think he's a great role model." We brought these guys to New York and they've done very well. At least two-thirds of our magazine is written by freelancers.

□ **What sparks your interest in a query or in a freelance writer?**
An idea that we haven't read before. News that nobody else would print. Also, references—editors who call to say this writer is a good guy.

□ **What do you look for in the clips?**
Wit. Good writing samples that show that the writer can write *Spy* prose.

□ **How much do you pay writers?**
We pay respectably but not extravagantly.

□ **Do you have pet peeves about writers?**
I hate when people call on the phone before I've had a chance to respond. Too many phone follow-ups are not cute.

Another pet peeve is when writers don't disclose the full truth. One writer forgot to mention that he was suing the company that he was writing about.

□ **What do you advise writers who want to be published in *Spy*?**
Read the magazine. The magazine speaks for itself. What's in there is what we think is good. Somebody who wants to write for *Spy* must be able to write something of comparable quality and attitude. If you like the magazine, propose topics that our readers will want to read.

□ **Are there any other keys to breaking in at *Spy*?**
A genuine interest in talking to our readers and a willingness to do anything to make them laugh and teach them something. We don't mind people who are willing to chance appearing sophomoric. We're very sentimental about people who make us laugh.

□ **You are editor in chief of *Psychology Today*, *Spy*, and *Mother Earth News*. How do you handle all of that?**
People would argue that it's a difficult job. What I say is, "It's the same material."

ABOUT THE AUTHOR

Judy Mandell is the author of numerous feature articles, with subjects ranging from horse-drawn carriages to how to get published, for major magazines and newspapers. Her books include *Magazine Writer's Nonfiction Guidelines* (McFarland & Co.), *Fiction Writers Guidelines* (McFarland & Co.), *Golden Opportunities: Deals & Discounts for Senior Citizens* (Thomassan-Grant), *The One Hour College Applicant* (Mustang Publishing—coauthored), and three computer handbooks. Her latest book, *Book Editors Talk to Writers* (John Wiley & Sons, 1995), was one of two books that launched the Wiley Books for Writers series. She has lectured about getting published and taught "Creative Approaches to Publishing" at the University of Virginia.

Mrs. Mandell is a graduate of Cornell University. She has two sons, one daughter, two daughters-in-law, and two grandsons. She lives with her husband, Jerry, two huge dogs, and lots of tropical fish in North Garden, Virginia (near Charlottesville).

Epilogue

Editors want good writers just as writers want good editors. But editors have the power to choose, so writers must write smart and play the game according to the rules.

It is my hope that by reading this book and heeding the advice of the editors, readers will get together with the magazine editors of their dreams and become happily published.